ME VS. ME

Jada Christine

DEDICATION

To my husband, best friend and life partner, RuQuan

Thank you for nurturing my faith and encouraging me to unbury this book to share it with the world. This testimony ended before meeting you, but it remains *alive* because of your courage that has rubbed off on me. I love you.

TABLE OF CONTENTS

ME vs. ME

PROLOGUE

ME VS. HER

> For they hated knowledge and chose not to fear the Lord. They rejected my advice and paid no attention when I corrected them. Therefore, they must eat the bitter fruit of living their own way, choking on their own schemes. For simpletons turn away from me—to death. Fools are destroyed by their own complacency.
>
> Proverbs 1:29–32 NLT

I don't want you to eat the bitter fruit of living your own way. I tried it once and it was *sickening*. From the moment we leave the wombs of our mothers, the world blasts our ears with messages like:

"Follow your heart."

"Chase your dreams."

"Walk in your truth."

"Believe in whatever makes you happy."

"Do what you know is good for you".

"You are perfect the way that you are. Don't change."

1

The central focus of all this is the self: self-guidance and self-service, which ultimately leads to self-centeredness and selfishness. Although it may not sound that way at first, it can be deceivingly inspiring, causing us to blindly follow it, hoping it will lead us to our destiny. I, too, fell into this trap. I listened to her—the voice inside me. I followed my gut feelings, the desires in my heart, and the distorted truth she created that seemed to work for her in her own world. Little did I realize that by feeding her power, she would later use it against me and take control of my spirit. Suddenly, there was no "I" and no "me." She completely dominated me, and I became enslaved to my own flesh.

We lived according to her agenda, doing whatever she desired. At first, it seemed harmless, until curiosity emerged, and she developed a new desire to pursue things outside of her self-designed "garden." She convinced me that we were just having innocent fun, so I placed my trust in her. I was veiled, spiritually blinded. She led me to a tree and fed me its forbidden fruits, and I remained completely unaware of how that fruit was manifesting in my life. To be frank, she was dragging me to hell. Her agenda was to live fast and die young, to operate in ignorance by believing everything she heard and consuming everything she was fed. She accepted everything as truth, except for the actual truth. The truth convicted her because it demonized the lifestyle of her and her friends. Growing up, I had been taught that the truth is simply the truth, regardless of differing opinions. However, as her slave, my voice didn't matter. She was in control, and she despised everything I stood for. Her dominion over me was slowly killing me.

Her "garden" represented the beautiful life God had placed her in, her "tree of knowledge of good and evil" symbolized the world, and her forbidden fruit was curiosity. Parents, pastors, and siblings had warned me to stay away from evil, just as God had warned Adam and Eve not to eat from the fruit. However, it appeared so enticing and harmless, just as the serpent had portrayed it to Eve. I couldn't resist. It didn't appear evil to me.

I listened to her for the same reasons Eve listened to the serpent and Adam listened to Eve. The devil knows how to make something that is bad for us seem good. Moreover, as humans, we are born into sin, and we have an innate desire for sin. We consistently give in to our own desires and our own understanding, ultimately leading us towards self-destruction.

If you are a follower of Jesus Christ, you understand how challenging the battle between the flesh and the spirit can be. It means to die to our flesh daily in order to live a spirit-led life and to allow God to renew our minds. Many people misunderstand that believers no longer desire to sin simply because they choose not to. However, the natural human desire remains and always will. Yet, we choose to suppress it and deny it out of reverence for God and for the sake of our spirits. If we don't, we risk spiritual death. Dying to self is a process of becoming new, allowing change to happen through obedience and discipline. It means saying no to ourselves when we want to engage in something we shouldn't and saying yes to what we know we should be doing, even when we don't want to.

It requires letting the Holy Spirit hold us accountable through conviction, and at times, it can feel like there are two opposing forces within us, pulling us in opposite directions…because there is. Dying to self means crucifying the fantasies that excite us, so we don't fall into sexual immorality. It could also mean saying no to going out with friends, even though it may leave us spending our nights alone watching TV. Sometimes it's as simple as waking up on time and going to work instead of staying in bed. It's a constant push and pull between these two desires within us—to do good or not to do good. Whether you are a believer or not, you and I both know of these daily battles.

It seems as if our flesh is against us. Is free will a trap? Why would someone choose to go to hell? Why are we tormented by this ongoing battle between the flesh and the spirit throughout life, knowing that the victor determines our fate? Some people may think that God sends people to hell, but in truth, it is we who decide, through our actions, where we will end up.

> I have discovered this principle of life—that when I want to do what is right, I inevitably do what is wrong. I love God's law with all my heart. But there is another power within me that is at war with my mind. This power makes me a slave to the sin that is still within me. Oh, what a miserable person I am! Who will free me from this life that is dominated by sin and death? Thank God! The answer is in Jesus Christ our Lord. So you see how it is: In my mind I really want to obey God's law, but because of my sinful nature I am a slave to sin.
>
> Romans 7:21–25 NLT

We are so far from perfect, that God wiped out the entire planet in a massive flood, sparing only Noah and his family, to restore the goodness of His creation. Our predictability is so apparent that the Israelites' transformed an 11-day journey into a 40-year ordeal due to their lack of faith. Despite hearing about their mistakes repeatedly in church, we continue to fail to learn from them. Consequently, we find ourselves trapped in the same generational curses and perpetuating destructive cycles by ignorantly teaching our descendants to follow selfish ways.

God sent His son to save us from *ourselves*.

We cannot grasp the fact that we are simply His children and our Heavenly Father knows best. Instead, we question His authority and put our trust into our own limited knowledge. Despite our awareness of our inability to grasp His unfathomable ways, we choose to seek answers elsewhere. We reject, deny, and rebel against Him constantly without failure.

To humble ourselves and recognize our desperate need for a savior brings relief. It alleviates the pressure off those of us who believe we have everything figured out, and it allows those of us who were forced to mature early to regain our childlike innocence. It removes the burden of perfection and the expectation to always do things the right way. We make mistakes so frequently that we condemn ourselves with shame and guilt, often to the point of believing we are unworthy of life. However, we have a so loving Heavenly Father who showers us with endless grace and mercy, welcoming us into His arms after every stumble. He permits us to be perfectly imperfect in His presence while gently guiding us. His love for His children is so profound that He refuses to let us remain victims of our own ways. The one true remedy that saves us from our flesh is Jesus—Yeshua.

Once the Holy Spirit revealed to me that the only way to escape the destructive nature of my flesh was to live a spirit-led life, I began to take up my cross daily and put on the full armor of God to engage in this battle, rather than accepting defeat. I realized that I needed a savior because relying on my own judgment only led me down a path of destruction. Once she got out of control, only God could put her in check. She wouldn't listen to anyone, but every knee bows to the voice of God—yes, even her. He helped me confine her, and now I hear her cries every single day. Her time controlling my life was abruptly cut short, and she mourns the days when I obeyed her every command. As she remains imprisoned, she continues to lose her strength, and her cries became fainter, almost non-existent. She is silenced every time I pray and meditate on His word, she weakens with every moment I spend in worship, and she pleads for an opportunity to speak every time I proclaim His message.

She—my flesh—was heading towards the face of demons, and I blindly followed, only with a mutter of disapproval. How could I not see that she was plotting my demise right before my eyes? As a human being, I understand that I may still succumb to her ways, but I now serve a Savior who is greater than her. She has lost all custody over me, and I no longer belong to her. I am now a child of God, walking alongside my rightful guardian, embracing my true identity.

After searching for an escape in all the wrong places, I have finally found freedom from her, through Him.

Today, I stand here to share a contrary message to what social media bombards you with. It's not about us. This world does not revolve around us. We are cohabitants of Earth—brothers and sisters. Our lives are not our own. We have been strategically placed here by Someone far greater than us. We exist to serve Him and each other, and this is a life we cannot lead alone. We need a Higher Being—God—to look down upon us from His bird's eye view, seated in Heavenly places, and guide us through the unknown. We cannot see life the way He does, and although we may make "good" decisions, they may not always be the best decisions. If you desire a fulfilling life free from self-sabotage, self-defeat, self-inflicted strongholds, and self-destruction, you must no longer submit to yourself. Step outside of yourself and relinquish control to the Spirit—specifically, the Holy Spirit. The greatest obstacle in your life is you. We erect barriers that hinder us from moving forward, be it through our choices, the sins we are enslaved to, the false gods we serve, the company we keep, or our inability to execute and follow through on our goals.

We cannot live our lives to its optimal potential if we bear unresolved trauma, fears, pains, insecurities, and stagnancies. Moreover, trying to navigate our way out of these issues on our own is often futile, especially if we are the ones who've caused it. Even the world itself cannot offer a true solution, for the same reason: the world is often the cause. Our answer lies in The Father.

It is evident within human nature that we possess selfishness, weakness, ignorance, quick tempers, and even laziness. Yet, we still often make the argument that we are inherently good people. However, there is greater power in acknowledging our shortcomings rather than denying them. We'd only need to observe one child on this planet to see their inclination to do wrong and their need for correction. As adults, we are no different from children in this regard; the only distinction lies in the type of correction we receive. Just as children need to be taught not to bite their friends, we too sometimes need guidance to restrain our own tongues and not hurt people with our language. The need for correction in children does not diminish their lovability, and the same principle applies to us. It is the lack of correction in people's lives that has led to a world that appears heartless, merciless, and wicked. When we hurt ourselves through self-serving decisions driven by our fleshly desires, we inevitably end up hurting others. Hurt people, hurt people.

Let us put an end to this cycle. The transformation begins with you.

PART I

SERVING THE FLESH.

CHAPTER ONE

THE VEIL

> But the people's minds were hardened, and to this day whenever the old covenant is being read, the same veil covers their minds so they cannot understand the truth. And this veil can be removed only by believing in Christ. Yes, even today when they read Moses' writings, their hearts are covered with that veil, and they do not understand.
>
> 2 Corinthians 3:14–15 NLT

This veil mentioned in Corinthians could be described as the opposite of faith for believers, and many of us have experienced it. Faith is unwavering confidence and trust in God. During the time I was veiled, I placed my confidence solely in my own perceptions and understanding. I did not know better, so I did not do better. I was trapped in the bliss of ignorance. The "bliss" I lived in was a deceptive state that all humans have fallen into: sin. I believed my actions were good, but my definition of "good" was influenced by human standards and the world, rather than by God. To me, free will meant I had the right to do anything, regardless of whether it was beneficial or not. From my (limited) perspective, Christianity was the veil and believers were so blinded by their religion that they couldn't see the truth. I stood for nothing, therefore I fell for every deception.

I didn't always think this way. It began during my senior year of high school and fully developed in my first year of college. My senior year was one of my favorites, although it was cut short. I had finally emerged from a state of depression that had plagued me in the previous years, I grew my academic performance, and I joined student leadership. I **believed** in God, but I was very spiritually immature due to my lack of dedication to **understanding** God, and I only attended church because my mother insisted on it. I had Prom, Senior Night, College Decision Day, and Graduation Day right in front of me. Then, on March 13 of 2020, everything changed, marking the end of my senior year. The COVID-19 global pandemic abruptly disrupted my transition from childhood to young adulthood, stealing away six months of crucial experiences. I found myself crying every night once again, grieving the loss of my senior year.

The period of quarantine pushed me into various rabbit holes on social media that did me more harm than good. Ultimately it fed my flesh and led me to prioritize my worldly desires. I eventually succumbed to downloading TikTok, despite initially dismissing it as an app for young children, and I became instantly captivated. It exposed me to the ideas of New Age Spirituality, and I grew curious about concepts like manifestation, the power of the universe, and psychics offering tarot readings about the future. Unfortunately, I was completely unaware of the darkness that lay behind these practices. I identified as a novice activist, feminist, and spiritual enthusiast, convinced that I had discovered the light. I thought I was "woke", or enlightened, and I ignorantly embraced a carefree and open-minded spirit. I explored the possibilities and followed whatever sounded good to my heart.

Ironically, while claiming enlightenment, I began engaging in behaviors that I had to hide in the dark. I knew they were detrimental to me, which is why I kept them hidden. Although my mother still made me watch church services every Sunday on Facebook Live during the pandemic, I also fed my spirit with other influences. I began watching pornography every single night, only to pray before bed as if God hadn't witnessed the whole ordeal. I mindlessly scrolled through social media for hours, absorbing countless ideas and studying them, all the while growing convinced that my pastor was out of touch with reality. Graduation, which was just months away, lost its significance in my eyes. I was prepared for a new beginning.

All my older sisters had attended college in the Bay Area of Northern California, and I desired the same experience. Whenever I thought about college, I daydreamed about meeting a basketball player who would become my first boyfriend, forming a close-knit group of black friends, and embracing my independence. COVID-19 threatened my fantasy, and I felt utterly helpless. Although school would be conducted online, I still longed to live in the dorms for that quintessential "college experience." After shedding many tears, my dad reassured me that he would make the move happen. So, I began to plan out what college life would truly be like for me.

My pastor often referred to college as the "devil's playground," and it wasn't until later that I truly grasped the meaning behind those words. I was brimming with anticipation as I had packed my bags a month prior to move-in day. I "stacked my coins" braiding as much hair as I possibly could in order to buy myself everything I wanted in my dorm room, and to have a little spending money on campus. Silly enough, I even checked out the Division I Basketball roster to find a potential love interest like TikTok told me to. Eager to immerse myself in the college experience, I introduced myself on the University's Class of 2024 Instagram page. Before I knew it, I found myself in a massive group chat with other young students who looked like me, all preparing to embark on our college journey. In our group chat we helped each other figure out registration, got to know each other, and laughed at silly memes. However, we also had conversations that revolved around parties, smoking, drinking, sex, and all the other things young people engage in during college. Through these discussions, I quickly realized how sheltered my upbringing had been—not necessarily a bad thing, but I couldn't hide my naiveté. Up to that point my "experience" consisted of sipping on my mother's wine a few occasions and harboring a secret addiction to porn. I found these conversations intriguing, and I spent hours texting my new friends in the group chat. I bombarded them with questions, seeking to catch up with them:

"What's the difference between a bong, a pre-roll, and a blunt?"

"Why can't you mix light and dark liquor?"

"What's the difference between Sativa and Indica?"

They all wanted to be the one who would initiate me into this world by giving me my first experience hitting a blunt or chugging a can of Four Loko down my throat at parties. I can't even blame it on peer pressure because I shamelessly wanted to be included in it. I entertained and encouraged it even though my older sister had warned me about the dangers of getting caught up in the college lifestyle. But when everyone around you is venturing into uncharted territory, it becomes increasingly difficult to refrain from joining in, especially when you lack a strong belief system.

Now, I understand why my pastor referred to college as the devil's playground. The enemy capitalizes on the foolishness and curiosity of youth. While everyone is moving in one direction, trying to stay on the straight and narrow path feels like swimming against the powerful wave currents of an ocean. It's no wonder that slipping off the narrow path becomes all too easy. The path of righteousness can be isolating, and the scriptures themselves describe it as arduous. In the college environment, it becomes even more challenging. The path to destruction is wide and inviting, with everyone encouraging us to follow along. But as our mothers say, "If all your friends jump off a cliff, would you jump too?" Well, I wouldn't, but my flesh certainly would, and that's precisely what happened every time I senselessly followed the crowd during my first year of college.

Move-in day filled me with indescribable joy. Stepping onto campus for the first time sent an exhilarating rush through my body, and I could finally envision myself entering a new era of my life. I was assigned to room number 1111 on the Black Scholars Floor, and I couldn't help but interpret it as a sign from God that I was exactly where I needed to be. Or was it the universe communicating with me? Or perhaps God and the universe were one and the same? I no longer knew for certain, but what I did know was that I felt excited to be there. Right after settling into my room and saying goodbye to my parents, I met up with a few girls from the group chat. We bonded over discussions about our zodiac signs, explored the campus together, and ended our first night by enjoying boba drinks downtown.

The next morning, I embarked on a self-guided tour of the campus. Unfortunately, due to the pandemic I didn't get an opportunity to tour before moving in. The weather was picture-perfect, with just the right amount of sunshine and a gentle breeze swaying gracefully through the palm trees. Unsure of which direction to take, I stumbled upon the school's Olympic Black Power Statue. I found a bench nearby and settled down, savoring the moment while enjoying a refreshing cup of iced coffee from Philz.

As I absorbed the surroundings, the group of basketball players I had scouted pre-move-in strolled by, and I immediately recognized them. Though I couldn't get a good look at them, I noticed one of them, noticing me.

ANGEL OF LIGHT

The devil's appearance is not so obvious. He doesn't often blatantly approach us donning horns, sharp teeth, and a fiery tail like cartoon depictions would suggest. He's much more cunning than that and his tactics are far more insidious. The Bible warns us that he disguises himself as an angel of light (2 Corinthians 11:14). He works behind the scenes of seemingly good things, tempting us to idolize them above God, thus leading us astray. Self-help concepts, motivational speakers, and the pursuit of being a "high-value" individual, for instance, are not inherently bad and can actually be helpful in certain situations. Yet, the devil has deceived many into believing that these positive things will serve as their saviors. However, it's important to discern that not every good thing is a "God thing." God's desire is for us to wholeheartedly follow Him and Him alone. The devil, in contrast, employs various strategies to hinder us from doing so. He may tempt us to follow a god that has no true spiritual power, get us to create a god out of a simple thing by idolizing it, or make us into the god of our own lives. Emphasis on the lowercase g's.

> Make sure that the light you think you have is not actually darkness.
>
> Luke 11:35 NLT

Or perhaps he desires to deceive us into believing in something that contradicts God, yet promises similar outcomes. Take, for instance, New Age Spirituality or other religions. Upon closer examination of their underlying concepts, we find that they encompass numerous biblical principles such as love, faith, positivity, hope, and a desirable afterlife. However, they remove the one true God from the equation, diverting our faith towards something else. Ironically, Christianity is arguably the most ridiculed religion in the United States. While Christians in America may not face the same level of persecution as in other countries, we encounter significant levels of hatred, objection, mockery, and judgment due to our controversial beliefs.

Those who are veiled often remain unaware of the danger they are in. It becomes challenging to save someone who firmly believes they do not require salvation, and it is equally difficult to convince someone to embrace the truth when they harbor a deep-seated hatred towards it. I can definitely understand, being I was in that position once before. My first year of college I made myself my god. It all began innocently enough when my friends, whom I believed would never intentionally or unintentionally harm me, introduced me to marijuana. I had the idea it would take away my social anxiety and provide a sense of enjoyment. Similarly, I started seeking solace in tarot readings, hoping that foreknowledge of the future would instill hope within me. I even hopelessly pursued relationships thinking "love" would be my savior during my darkest moments. Yet, all of these pursuits turned out to be nothing but a deceitful facade. I had been warned that these things would not save me; in fact, they would bring danger upon me. However, it was my own idea of light before I got to know Christ for myself. The light in which I believed turned out to be utter darkness.

THE ILLUSION

In the midst of this college lifestyle, I had a conversation with my older sister that I will never forget. She told me about Christ and warned me about the things I was doing but I specifically told her,

"I love God. I'm just doing me right now."

I now look back with the understanding that she was trying to introduce me to the one and only Savior I needed, but at the moment I didn't know I needed Him and frankly, I didn't want Him. The only thing I wanted was for the conversation to be over. I felt attacked and judged even though she was only projecting love. She loved me so much that she cared enough for my soul to tell me the truth, but the truth hurt.

> Our lives are a Christ–like fragrance rising up to God. But this fragrance is perceived differently by those who are being saved and by those who are perishing. To those who are perishing, we are a dreadful smell of death and doom. But to those who are being saved, we are a life–giving perfume. And who is adequate for such a task as this?
>
> 2 Corinthians 2:15–16 NLT

How could I confess my love for God but announce myself as my own master in the same breath? Those few words I spoke told her everything she needed to know. God had exposed my truth to her and nothing was hidden. Her light revealed my darkness and I felt impermissibly vulnerable and convicted. It was the same feeling I get now as I read the sharp word of God that cuts between my soul and spirit and exposes my innermost thoughts and desires (Hebrews 4:12).

I saw the life she lived, and what she described as freedom in her life looked like shackles to me. We were playing for two different teams, had two different agendas, and had two different ideas of winning. The thought of discipline, self-control, and even abstaining from sex until marriage looked crippling even though I was a virgin who would generally call myself a "good person". I thought I was the one that was truly free by doing whatever I wanted to do whenever I wanted to do it, but I was only a slave to my bad decisions that I thought were good. We cannot be the person who defines what is good and what is bad in our lives when we live in a world that we didn't create. That's like being the kid that disobeys the rules in their mother's house but continuously chooses to believe that they're not wrong for doing it. This is not our house, and we must live by His rules. There is no way to "sin responsibly."

With a veil over our hearts, we fail to see that we often work against ourselves, lacking the understanding that many of the things we advocate for are actually trying to destroy us. Every belief or practice that is idolized above God shares the same agenda, whether it manifests as holistic living and motivational speaking or blatant sorcery. Their goal is to create division between us and our Heavenly Father.

> Rebellion is as sinful as witchcraft, and stubbornness as bad as worshiping idols. So because you have rejected the command of the Lord, he has rejected you as king.
>
> 1 Samuel 15:23 NLT

STANDING FOR NOTHING = FALLING FOR EVERYTHING

As believers, we are called to stand for one thing and one thing only. That is the truth. There is no room for double-mindedness or lukewarmness, as they signify a lack of true belief. It is impossible to serve two masters. If we claim to follow Christ but wholeheartedly embrace everything the world tells us, allowing ourselves to be influenced by everything we watch or listen to, then we have failed to exercise discernment and stand firm in our convictions. This applies not only to music, TV shows, and public figures but also to pastors who do not speak the truth and mislead many. To truly believe in the truth, we must diligently seek and know the truth. The Word says that God's people perish for a lack of knowledge (Hosea 4:6). We must be able to identify the lies surrounding us so that we do not fall into continuous traps of deception. If we gather in church and proclaim ourselves as followers of Jesus, yet blend in with the world by engaging in the same activities, we become no different from the world and, in fact, mislead them.

The world does not have a consistent foundation to believe in or hold on to. In Christ, we find peace, love, prosperity, protection, guidance, correction, fulfillment, joy, and more—all in one place. The world, on the other hand, searches for these things in various places, hoping to find the answers, but they fail, therefore they fall for everything. They even believe in multiple things that contradict each other without realizing it. During my time in college, I called myself a Christian, yet I believed in New Age Spirituality and relied on my own understanding—two things that rebel God.

Reflecting on that period, I realize how I spread myself thin among different ideologies, ultimately leaving myself unfulfilled each time. I sought most of the things mentioned above in getting in a relationship, but the one relationship I truly needed was with Christ. I searched for the rest by experimenting with drugs, partying, pornography, music, and New Age spirituality, believing they would provide what I was looking for, but they only made things worse.

The veil that covered my heart rendered me spiritually unreachable. It was only through Christ that I found liberation from the chains that my flesh had bound me in.

CHAPTER TWO

THE SERPENT.

The enemy is ruthless and takes advantage of those who are veiled. His efforts do not cease against Believers simply because we know the truth. Instead, he relentlessly pursues us, placing targets on our backs, because he is aware that our belief in Jesus doesn't remove our human frailty and weakness of the flesh. History repeats itself, as seen in the deception of Eve, who in turn, deceived Adam. Similarly, the world falls prey to the enemy's temptations, and now they seek to draw us into their midst, whether intentionally or unintentionally. Despite God's warning about the "tree of knowledge of good and evil" and its forbidden fruits, we find ourselves unable to resist consuming them.

FORBIDDEN FRUIT

For us, forbidden fruits are not the green apples we find in grocery stores. They represent the actions we engage in under the cover of darkness, attempting to conceal them in the light. These are the acts we are cautioned against, yet in the face of temptation, we question whether they are truly wrong. They appear enticing and pleasurable, but deep down, we know they are not. They are the detrimental habits we cling to for so long that we grow comfortable with them, convincing ourselves they are good. The world may have normalized and accepted these behaviors over time, but God's stance on them remains unchanged.

I could sit here and name every single one of our forbidden fruits but that's not necessary. What we do in secret remains between us and God until it is exposed to the light. Forbidden fruits, much like the devil himself, present themselves as delicious and gratifying. However, as we consume them, expecting to find satisfaction and fullness, they take a piece of us. We believe that indulging in forbidden fruit will provide us with revolutionary knowledge or fill the void within us. We partake in these actions because we are spiritually hungry creatures, and when we are not satisfied by the things of God, the things of the world become appetizing. Suddenly, pornography or engaging in casual sex with people through platforms like Tinder or Instagram appear as tantalizing as a juicy hamburger with a side of fries. Smoking marijuana seems as enticing as a five-star lobster meal with mashed potatoes and steak. Partying all night and getting drunk, all for the sake of projecting a fun-filled life on Instagram (despite the battle with depression behind closed doors), appears as glorious as a Thanksgiving dinner accompanied by the finest red wine. Yet, in reality, it is akin to devouring a stale bag of Hot Cheetos, leading to hours spent on the toilet and a trip to the emergency room to get your stomach pumped. In other words, it deceives us, wasting our time, leaving us in tears of heartbreak or shame, exhausted, hungover, and sinking further into depression. The allure of Hot Cheetos lies in their addictive nature, even though we regret eating them every time. We continue to purchase them repeatedly, until they begin corroding the lining of our stomachs, causing a larger health issue that only Jesus could heal. This is how intentionally living in sin effects our spirits.

(Side note: our bodies are temples physically _and_ spiritually. Let's take care of them both. God can do more with us outside of the hospital).

We often find ourselves grappling with chronic anxiety and depression, unable to comprehend why they persist, all the while indulging in the same forbidden fruit that only exacerbate our struggles. We question why we struggle to maintain stable and healthy relationships, whilst repeatedly gravitating towards individuals who mirror past patterns. Over time, we start feeling as though our issues are insurmountable, leading us to abandon hope for healing because we fail to perceive a way out. Yet, the answer is often right before our eyes: **we need to put an end to our detrimental habits.** Sadly, by the time we realize this truth, we have become so attached to our forbidden fruit that we adamantly refuse to let it go. We engage in a futile bargaining game with God, pleading for healing and deliverance while continuing to consume the fruit right in His presence, relying solely on His grace and mercy. However, such prayers lack vitality. Faith without works is dead. We must have faith that He can heal us while simultaneously demonstrating faith in His ability to grant us the strength and determination to relinquish the destructive habits that hinder our progress. It is imperative that we actively cooperate with Him in this transformative journey.

During my time in high school, I endured a two-year battle with anxiety and depression that weighed heavily on me day and night. Life seemed like a hazy blur during that period. It was kicking my behind. I had transferred to a different school in my sophomore year for a different basketball coach who could hopefully get me into college for free, and a fancy education program. Ironically, I didn't stick with either. Although I had a remarkable coach and an undefeated junior varsity basketball season, I was plagued by performance anxiety, which eventually drove me away from the team. Concurrently, depression crept into my life. I struggled to make friends, and the boy I was crushing on never acknowledged my existence. I was a popular loner. People knew of me but they didn't know me. To me, and to many other young folks, these things felt like the end of the world. It was hard leaving behind classmates I had known since kindergarten. My academic performance plummeted from straight A's to B's, then C's, and ultimately D's.

My hoodie stayed on, my door stayed closed, and my face was frozen with a frown. I was sobbing to sleep every other night, sending prayers up to God, and I felt utterly lost as a confused and emotionally wounded teenager. The only way I knew how to express my pain was through my spam account on Instagram—a common coping mechanism for many of my peers at the time. We snapped pictures of ourselves crying and publicized our pain to our 20 to 30 "finsta" friends, hoping for some form of help, only to realize people were just going to comment "same" and keep scrolling. During this time I vividly remember my grandmother's constant remark of, "Jada, you just don't seem like my Jada anymore." My parents seemed to walk on eggshells around me and I felt like my sadness was a burden to everyone, so I isolated myself. What I failed to realize at the time was that my struggle was not a mental health battle but it was a spiritual battle. I surrounded myself with friends who battled with depression, I immersed myself in music that glorified and romanticized mental health issues, I evaded my pain by immersing myself in social media, inadvertently nourishing it like pernicious weeds, and I continuously spoke negative words over myself. Sadly, I lacked the awareness to recognize it as a spiritual battle that could be fought. I viewed it solely through my physical eyes, casting myself as a victim in the process. I clung to those friendships because of my loyal nature, I was convinced that the music was my source of healing, I considered social media my "emotional outlet," and I repeated negative self-talk as if they were affirmations:

"I'm in a slump and I can't get out of it."

"Ima walking L."

"Bro nobody likes me. I'm just gonna be lonely forever."

"I'll always be like this. I won't change."

"No matter how hard I try I still suck."

"My whole mood is confused. I don't know how to feel about anything."

"I naturally isolate myself from everybody."

"I stay being taken for granted, underestimated, and overlooked. It don't make a difference if I'm in anyone's life or not. Y'all still gon be good."

These quotes are all old posts in my Snapchat memories from that time. Not only did I think and say these things, but I also posted them on social media. I thought I was releasing my pain, but instead, I found myself meditating on it and feeding it. What I thought was strengthening me was actually weakening me.

As my weariness with school grew, so did my weariness with church. I stopped reading my Bible, I barely understood it though, and all I wanted to do was sleep in. I'm pretty sure I was angry at God. Church seemed silly to me, and for the first time, I started questioning what I had been blindly following my whole life. I couldn't comprehend why people would get so emotional, or why my pastor would passionately scream during sermons. It was as if a seed had been left unwatered. While I received spiritual nourishment every Sunday, I failed to back it up with intentional time spent with God. Being young, I didn't truly grasp the significance of it. My intentions were good; I had faith in God to guide me out of darkness. However, my lack of understanding created distance during this time. I spiritually perished due to my lack of knowledge. If I wanted God's help, I realized I needed to nurture the seeds my pastor was planting within me every Sunday. Unfortunately, those seeds were falling among thorns.

My parents noticed my distance. Not my distance from God, but the distance I placed between myself and the whole family. Their concern only made me feel fragile and insecure, helpless.

I asked myself, "If my parents who I've relied on my entire life can't take away this pain, then who can?"

My emotions often manifested as anger toward them. One day, I saw our pastor pull into the driveway, and I wondered, "Why is *he* here?" Looking back, I praise God for his obedience and proactive efforts. He didn't do it for me; he did it for the Lord. My parents insisted that I talk to him. In my head, I was angry. What he said didn't offer much solace, but I also didn't provide him with much to work with. I had already convinced myself that he wouldn't be able to help me, so I was cold to him. I assumed my parents had invited him over to talk to me, but a few years later, they revealed that during that time he said he "saw something on me" and asked my parents for permission to speak with me. I was shocked. Over the years, I have heard him say the same thing to my sisters,

"I saw something on you."

And every time, he was right. Something was wrong. That discerning ability is a gift directly from the Holy Spirit. After our family conversation, I went right back up to my room, closed the door, and cried. Nothing helped.

BROAD PATH

You can enter God's Kingdom only through the narrow gate. The highway to hell is broad, and its gate is wide for the many who choose that way.

Matthew 7:13 NLT

Mental health struggles in teens are a very real issue. The hearts and minds of teens are fragile and vulnerable. My mother also dealt with anxiety and when I confided in her about having panic attacks, she shared some valuable advice given to her by her therapist on how to conquer it.

"Figure out what you're anxious about, find the root of the issue, and talk yourself down," she said.

I was able to de-escalate my anxiety as it was actively taking place and I gradually was able to overcome the panic attacks. I offered the same advice to my best friend at the time, as we were both a couple of anxious and depressed teens. However, with hindsight, I now realize that her burdens were much heavier than mine. Her healing required more than just a self-help tip, and it broke my heart. All I could do in that situation was pray for her, and so I did. Although I didn't know how to pray aloud for someone, I decided to write down a prayer for her one day during lunchtime.

Years later, when we were in college, we found ourselves discussing our mental health once again. This conversation led me to pen another prayer, which I felt was not only meant for her but also for myself.

Dear Heavenly Father,

First and foremost, forgive me for all my sins that I've done knowingly and unknowingly. I am young and can't see what You see. Hold me accountable for my actions, because that's the only way I will grow. Mature me spiritually and mentally. Let me pray this prayer over myself with the God Given authority You have given me over every single spiritual attack and over all worldly things. Holy Spirit, remind me to equip myself as I go to war against depression, anxiety, worldly things and _____________ every single day. Remind me that your word, prayer and worship are the most powerful weapons I can use in this war. Lord go before me in every battle and fight for me. Fight for my purpose, my emotions, my mental well-being, and every single detail in my life because these all matter to You and I. Remind me that when I'm in Your presence, I can be everything that I am. That I can come to You with all the chaos in my life and You can clean it all up for me if I just let You in. Nothing I feel or go through is too messy for You to clean up. I believe in Your power over my life more than I believe in the power of anxiety, depression and fear. As a matter of fact, they have no power. In the name of Jesus, I am free from all bondage spiritually and I will say it over and over again until I feel like I have been set free physically! Lord lead me to the people You want me to meet and the places You want me to go because I want it all. Close every door that I could have possibly opened with my actions and save me from my own destruction. In the bible it says that people ruin their own lives with foolishness and then get angry at the Lord, but help me to make wise decisions that change my life for the better. Allow me to experience the overwhelming peace that comes, when I come into Your presence. Remind me to cling to that feeling and hold onto it like my life depends on it because it does. Hold my hand in every single moment. When I feel alone physically, remind me that I am never alone spiritually. Do not let me become naive to the enemy's tricks. Do not let me become distracted by the world's chaos. Do not let me become tired of doing good. Please God, do not let me fall. Please God, hold my hand through it all. Help me to remember that Your ways are higher than my ways and when I don't understand what I'm going through I just have to trust You. You will use my pain, my hurt, and my chaos and mold it into Your peace, Your promises, and Your plan for my life. Give me discernment in every moment against things and people that are from You and things and people that have been sent to destroy me. Let me experience victory over my struggles and let me see just how good You are. I have seen what You have done for others and God I want it all. Give me the faith to trust in You when I don't feel You, or see where You're working. Remind me that You are my Father and You aren't angry with me. Your correction is love and You're just happy that I'm here. You're happy to hear my voice. You're happy to hear my praise. You're happy to see me keep pushing through it all even when I don't want to. You are proud of my small victories like getting out of bed when I don't feel like it and talking to You when I don't even know what to say. I do not accept depression or anxiety over my life which the enemy has been trying to use against me. I deny it all. I place my identity in being Your precious beloved child and in Your plan for my life only. I thank You for Your grace and Your love. I thank You for holding me in Your arms and keeping me here. Thank You for keeping me God, because my existence is just enough proof to show that You have greater plans and that You can take me places I have never imagined for myself...

In the name of the Father, the Son, and the Holy Spirit I pray.

AMEN.

Not much has changed in my situation since high school, but my perspective has undergone a transformation. As I write this, I still don't have many friends, I'm still single, and I spend most of my free time alone. In retrospect, this makes sense now with the understanding that as believers, we are called to be set apart. However, during that time, there was a spiritual attack that I failed to recognize that came from associating myself with those on the broad path. They never appeared to be lonely. They were always surrounded by large crowds, hundreds of likes and comments, and always had a love interest. I desired to be part of the world, to be friends with those who indulged in foolishness and appeared happy, and I despised being alone. God saw something that my peers were struggling with, something I couldn't see, and He kept me away from them. Yet, I still tried to imitate them. I listened to their music, posted what they posted, mimicked their behavior on social media, and adopted their way of speaking because I didn't truly understand my identity in Christ. I was attempting to fit into a mold that wasn't meant for me, which resulted in social anxiety, confusion about my identity, and depression stemming from loneliness. I isolated myself from the only people who truly understood me at that time—my family. I was searching for community on the broad path.

Depression haunted me, but I couldn't pinpoint its source. It was all a blur. All I remember is drowning my sorrow each night, blasting SZA, H.E.R., J. Cole, and crying out in prayer until the pain subsided. In hindsight, I should have realized that indulging in melancholic music only would amuse my pain.

Without identifying the root cause of my depression, I continued to seek approval from the world during my college years. I found myself conforming to the actions of others, disregarding boundaries, and listening to every voice around me. I was surrounded by individuals who lacked direction, and I, like a blind person, followed their lead. I didn't stand on one truth, therefore I accumulated a number of lies and proclaimed it as "my truth." My truth was nothing but a massive deceitful lie. This path seemed easy, but I was oblivious to the fact that it led to the death of my spirit. My truth convinced me that I would reach Heaven and reconcile with the Father by serving myself over Him. However, anything that promises access to Heaven and reconciliation with the Father through anything other than Christ is a falsehood. I had made myself a god. The master I served was me.

> Jesus told him, "I am the way, the truth, and the life. No one can come to the Father except through me."
>
> John 14:6 NLT

Deep down, I knew that my lifestyle did not align with God's approval, but my peers, who were also on this broad path, validated and reinforced my lifestyle. They were also disguised as "light," but they too were blinded just as I was. They advertised friendship, fun, and popularity, and I bought into these relationships, treating them as if they were my family—the only way I knew how. Unfortunately, I was left betrayed and heartbroken. As a human, I desired certain "forbidden fruits," but I refrained from partaking until they were offered to me. Eventually, I became the one who would tempt others.

"Come smoke with me."

"Let's go to this party."

"Take a shot with me!"

"Have you heard this new song?"

My flesh desired sin, and I would hear a still, small voice in my head saying "no." But if I could get validation from others while engaging in these actions, the "yes" from the world silenced the internal "no." I longed to fulfill these desires and I needed an accomplice, a partner in crime who would agree with me as my flesh led me down this destructive path. Only then would the voice in my head, which opposed me and condemned my lifestyle, be silenced. In college, I encountered numerous individuals who were also searching for an accomplice. They used me solely to validate their own wrongdoings, and I, in turn, learned to do the same to others. However, these relationships lacked true friendship and intimate connection. Once I left behind my old ways and turned to Christ, I discovered that I no longer shared anything in common with them. Those friendships were built on lies. We were co-dependent, relying on each other to sustain our toxic behaviors. Suddenly, the encouragement to partake in the familiar, enjoyable activities we used to engage in sounded like the serpent tempting Eve to eat the forbidden fruit.

Interestingly, those who invited me to join them did not seem to comprehend the harm of what they were doing. I reasoned that if they were aware that their actions led to death, they would not encourage others to partake, right? However, I realized that both they and I were fully aware of our self destructive habits.

> They know God's justice requires that those who do these things deserve to die, yet they do them anyway. Worse yet, they encourage others to do them, too.
>
> Romans 1:32 NLT

The broad path is easy to walk on because it is the path everyone treads upon. It is effortless to be swayed by the winds of societal norms and to ride the currents of culture. It is comfortable to blend in with the crowd and never experience loneliness. It is convenient to imitate the world and follow the person closest to us. It is so tempting to listen to anyone and do everything they suggest, simply going with the flow. However, we must remember that the path of ease is not necessarily the path we should choose.

CHAPTER THREE

ABANDONMENT.

The enemy doesn't want us to follow his wicked ways for him to be a loving father, who cares for and watches over his children. He's like a deadbeat daddy. We can always count on him to be the exact opposite of God. He raises his children in toxic environments, wanting them to struggle just as he does. Satan knows that his eternal home is hell, and he wants to take everyone down with him to keep him company. He tries to bring us in so that he can abandon us to his fate. His mindset is that if he can't win, then no one can. Once he has us shackled to serving our own flesh, indulging in forbidden fruits, or serving him, he leaves us to face the consequences our actions have brought upon us. The devil puts us into a prison where we have nothing but time to reflect upon our lives and become filled with regret. Then he tries to condemn us with the idea that we will spend our lives in this prison, that we are damned and unforgivable. He tries to convince us that there is absolutely no way out and that no one is there to help. But here's a reminder: all he can do is lie.

Whether we come to realize the reality of light and darkness or not, we all experience pain from the world. It's part of the human condition. I learned this the same way a child does when they're told to stay away from a hot stove. They touch the stove out of curiosity, get burned, and never touch it again. I got burned. Real bad. Even when I impulsively desire to give in, hoping for a different outcome, I'm left with another burn and the same sense of shame. <u>Some people learn from their wounds the first time, some will learn after a few times, and some never learn at all.</u> We have a strong addiction to the world, especially those who don't know that there is a God who exists outside of this world and can transform lives. We continue to seek healing from the same sources and follow the same path, even though we know the outcome. As a result, our wounds become larger, issues take root within us even deeper, and more problems are swept under our rugs. Yet we can't help it. We feel obligated to remain loyal to the people and things that aren't good for us simply because they have been around for so long.

> As a dog returns to its vomit, so a fool repeats his foolishness.
>
> Proverbs 26:11 NLT

Being wounded by the world is a humbling experience. Reality checks have a way of putting us in a child's place, even though we may be much older. It can be embarrassing to realize that we need correction and help, just like children do. While most of us can manage to take care of ourselves physically, when it comes to inward issues, we are all still children in the eyes of God, and we always will be. No amount of time and experience on this Earth can measure up to God's sovereign wisdom. He knows everything. Seeing the consequences of our lifestyles manifest right in front of us makes us feel foolish. It's a reminder that, despite our age, we are still children. Our flesh doesn't "know it all," and this world won't save us from our flesh either. We make mistakes throughout our lives, but as we grow older, these mistakes can lead to life-altering or even life-threatening consequences. The world doesn't care about ensuring that adults are doing well. So, who will take care of us? Certainly not the enemy, and certainly not ourselves.

The problems we create in our lives are often difficult to eliminate, and definitely not as enjoyable as the process of creating them. This world is cold. These wounds inflicted upon us weigh heavily, leaving us feeling dejected and adopting a "woe is me" attitude. The burden of these wounds shifts our perspectives, causing us to perceive our circumstances as exalted over any good things in life. The violence, racism, poverty, and wars around us serve as evidence that something wicked is at work in this world. And no less, the cold hearts, pride, greediness, and shallowness in our culture show the same evil. No matter the measure, the pain that directly affects each of our own lives, has an eye-opening effect on our perception of the world. We finally begin to comprehend the reality of both light and darkness, but not everyone realizes that the origins of these forces are far greater than what is bad and what is good. There are spiritual dimensions in action, manifesting in the physical realm. The inner wounds we carry are the result of poor choices made in the physical world, influenced by our fleshly desires, that ultimately attack us both internally and externally. This deep-seated pain and sorrow, invisible to the naked eye, requires a spiritual healer. The chaos we experience in our lives is part of a spiritual battle for our souls, and to emerge victorious, we need the "big G" God on our side.

Our stories are hardly ever original, as all humans share relatable experiences. When we share our testimonies, hope is kindled in the hearts of the hopeless. Those who have felt invisible begin to feel seen as we give voice to our stories. Through vocalizing our experiences, we discover the power in recognizing how far God has brought us. We often underestimate the influence, worth, and value of our own pain, thinking that it pales in comparison to someone else's. The truth is that all pain hurts, whether it be a minor heartbreak, the loss of a loved one, or unfortunate circumstances.

> ...if someone asks about your hope as a believer, always be ready to explain it. But do this in a gentle and respectful way. Keep your conscience clear. Then if people speak against you, they will be ashamed when they see what a good life you live because you belong to Christ.
>
> 1 Peter 3:15–16 NLT

It's pretty tough making friends in college during a global pandemic when everyone is quarantined in their dorm rooms without roommates. One night, I was hanging out with the girls I had met up with on move-in day. Most of us lived on the Black Scholars floor, so we decided to knock on everyone's doors on the floor to meet the other black students. Our dorm building looked like it hadn't been renovated since the school was founded in 1857. The walls of the hallway were painted in an outdated yellow shade that resembled the walls of a smoker's home, and there was a worn-out denim blue color on all the door frames. There was no air conditioning, and the oversized heaters hanging over each door didn't even work. As we made our way through puzzled faces and gained a few more Instagram followers, we encountered a group of guys on the floor just as we were about to leave. I had always been somewhat reserved around boys, but my friends instantly connected with them.

I had never been part of a co-ed, all-black friend group before, and I thought that I had met friends I would have forever. I tend to think that way due to my naive nature, and unfortunately, I always end up getting hurt because of it. We did everything together—grocery shopping at Target, exploring the city of San Francisco, doing homework, swiping on Tinder to see the campus cuties, and more. Yet sometimes, it felt like they were the ones doing it together and I was just their observer. I constantly felt invisible around them, from being asked to capture group photos of them without me in them, to watching the guys bring bouquets of flowers to all the other girls in the group showing appreciation for their friendship, without even looking at me. I was a ghost, yet I couldn't help but to continue to come around them hoping they'd treat me differently. They excluded me from activities, inviting me at the last minute, and even when we were all together, I struggled to find my place in the conversations. It saddened me that I couldn't form a strong bond with the only other black people on campus. I wasn't as experienced with things as them. They were all from LA or the Bay area and I was from the suburbs. Many of their conversations were foreign to me, highlighting my innocence and the cultural differences between us. I remember one of the guys referring to me as a "sweetheart," which I'd been called my whole life, leaving me uncertain whether to embrace my wholesomeness or feel disappointed by it. After much inner turmoil and self-reflection on whether I wanted to be alone by myself or alone within a group, I eventually chose to distance myself from them for the sake of my own self-worth.

My first college party turned out to be a little odd and it went south quickly. I hesitate to even call it a party. During the pandemic, we weren't allowed to visit each other's dorms, but one particular girl, who later became the betrayer in this tale (let's call her Judas), had different plans. Referring to her as Judas may seem dramatic, but unfortunately, she is the one who broke my trust in this story, and thus a pseudonym is necessary. Judas and I instantly connected due to our shared sense of humor. Like many other college girls, she identified as part of the LGBTQ+ community and had an unhealthy relationship with alcohol. Despite her flaws, I loved her, as she reminded me of a few friends from my past.

One evening, while my friends and I were talking with her in the quad, she informed us that she was having people over in her dorm. Even though I was dressed casually in sweatpants, a hoodie, with a headscarf on my edges, I decided to come. It started very casually with Judas and I creating silly TikToks, and before I knew it, I found myself kicking it back with 13 other kids in a shoebox sized dorm room sipping on White Claws.

I met someone that night who seemed like the male version of me, and we talked the whole time. We were both tall, came from the same suburban hometown, shared the Libra zodiac sign, and had similar cultural backgrounds. It was an enjoyable conversation until he became fixated on why I had never consumed alcohol or tried vaping. Fortunately, the resident advisor's interruption with loud banging on the door brought the conversation to an early end. Everyone, including myself, made a poor attempt to hide. Unfortunately, the situation quickly escalated when the cops arrived and informed us that they would have to inform our parents since some of us were underage and alcohol was present. One girl started crying uncontrollably, but I swiftly texted my mom to plead my case before the police could reach her. I assured her that I hadn't taken a single sip of alcohol, and it was the truth. Although I had no interest in alcohol at the time, I did have a curiosity about trying weed.

On another occasion, we all attended a kickback at a girl's house while her parents were away. This was my first experience at a real "party." The weather was chilly and windy, and I wore an auburn sweater paired with blue denim jeans I had grown out of that barely reached my ankles. Once I saw how the other girls were dressed and noticed that all the freshmen on the boys' basketball team were present, I immediately regretted my outfit choice. It was during this gathering that I met "Mr. Situationship", and my "partner in crime". I vividly recall Cardi B's "WAP" blaring from the speakers as everyone focused on making TikToks rather than dancing. The mingling scents of pizza, fruit punch, and vodka filled the room. It was also the night I got high for the first time. Ironically, my black friends wanted to metaphorically take my "weed virginity", but it ended up being the white girl I had just met that night who showed me more kindness than anyone else I had encountered on that campus. She had the sweetest spirit, kindest smile and looked like Barbie. We became a dynamic duo — smoke buddies, wearing matching Christmas pajamas, sneaking into her dorm room, creating TikToks for hours, and talking about boys. We were each other's favorite person on campus. During the kickback, we went outside to her car and took a few hits from her bong while hotboxing the car. The high set in once we returned inside and settled on the couch. Uncontrollable laughter overcame me, and I leaned over to my partner in crime and whispered, "I think I'm high." I remember looking over and making eye contact with the basketball player, who also appeared to be under the influence for the first time as well, only from alcohol. It only intensified my laughter. I went from spending most of my time with my black friends to constantly being with my two white friends — my partner in crime and Judas. Our favorite thing to do was to watch the Bachelorette together every week.

Flirting with guys was something I hadn't really done before, but under the influence, I felt the confidence to introduce myself, proudly proclaim that I was a hairstylist, and even engage in a spirited debate about whether pineapple belongs on pizza with one of the other players. It definitely does. That night, I acquired three new clients, and the cutest guy saved my number as "Jada The World's Best Braider," while Mr. Situationship and I exchanged Snapchats. I hate to admit it, but the validation I received bolstered my confidence.

(Side note for all of the girlies: If a man asks for your Snapchat, he's not tryna wife you up.)

Every time I went to their dorm to do their hair, I took my girlfriends with me. We all found at least one of them attractive, and whenever we would go everyone would become flirtatious. I could tell they had caught the guys' attention, but embarrassingly enough I still didn't know how to flirt. It kind of worked in my favor (if we don't count how things ended). Mr. Situationship saw their flirting as corny, and over time, he shot his shot with me. He was (dang near 7 feet) tall, dark, and slightly handsome.

One day, we all planned to go to the mall as a big group. It was on that day that I finally realized my black friends weren't really my friends. We had discussed going to the mall a few days prior, but no one gave me a specific time. As the day went on, I waited in my dorm, hoping to receive some information. Finally, I sent a text to inquire if we were still going, only to find out that they were already leaving at that moment. I hurriedly left my dorm, only to discover that they had invited the basketball players and there was "no room" for me anymore. They told me to squeeze into the car with the other boys, and as I got into the tiny car, I was greeted with annoyed faces. In that moment, I resolved that it would be the last time I would subject myself to such treatment. However, I was excited to see that the basketball players were there, and Mr. Situationship seemed glad to have me around too. When we arrived at the mall, I entered Urban Outfitters and came across some records. I decided to add "The Writings on the Wall" by Destiny's Child to my collection. As I walked out of the store, he was leaving Foot Locker, and I proudly showed off my new collectible to him. He was fascinated by the fact that I even had a collection. It must've left an impression on him because a few moments later, as we all walked towards the food court, he looked over at me and said, "You look kind of familiar."

Realizing that he was trying to flirt, I replied, "Me?"

"Yeah... I think I've seen you in my wallet... 'cause you a dime!"

I started blushing and couldn't help but let out my ugly laugh. I could tell his homeboy got second-hand embarrassment by the interaction, but I was flattered. It seemed like both of us were the oddballs of our friend groups. We shared the same taste in music, and we were a little weird in the eyes of our black friends. I had never been in any sort of relationship with a guy before, and I was curious about him.

From that day forward, it seemed like I always ran into him at the Dining Commons during breakfast. He teased me for getting orange juice every morning, and I playfully mocked him for choosing apple juice. I would flirt by asking for his playlist, inquiring about what it was like to play D1 basketball, and by being his hairstylist who touched up his two-strand twists. Eventually, his hair appointments became free and turned into casual hangouts.

On the night of my 18th birthday, the two of us took turns playing songs for each other while talking for hours after watching a scary movie. Our bond grew stronger due to our shared love and similar taste for music.

- "Poe Man's Dreams" by Kendrick Lamar

- "Part III" by Isaiah Rashad

- "A.W.O.L." by EARTHGANG

- "A Real Fly Love Song" by Merlaku Ra

He let me borrow his Dreamville hoodie, and we stayed up so late that I ended up unintentionally spending the night. We were lying down, watching TV, and I started feeling drowsy. Out of the blue, he turned off the TV, and without saying a word, we both headed to sleep. I had never had a sleepover with a guy before, but I felt an inner sense of happiness. The next morning, I woke up first, desperately needing to use the bathroom. Honestly, I don't think I had even slept because I was too nervous. As I crawled out of his bed and made my way to the bathroom, he must have woken up, confused about where I had gone. When I walked out of the bathroom, I saw him in the hallway, rubbing the sleep out of his eyes, looking for me. We spent the rest of the morning having breakfast together.

D1 athletes speak a universal language when it comes to girls, and every girl who's interested in D1 athletes tends to become blind to the red flags when they're interested in one. That language is simple: the barest minimum. If they're not genuinely interested, they give as little as possible. Unfortunately, I, as a person who tends to see the best in others, would often romanticize our moments together. However, the truth is, there was nothing extraordinary about our connection except for a few commonalities we shared.

Over time, I began to notice a significant number of Snapchats from other girls on his phone **(red flag #1)**. My lame excuse was that I wasn't in a rush to enter a relationship, and that we were merely friends so we could talk to whomever we pleased. I don't want to be the one to bring up race, but I noticed all the other girls were white. Honestly, it seemed like he was exploring his first relationship with a black girl when he met me.

There was no communication in this "situationship" so I sought validation for my theories on his intentions through numerous tarot readings on my TikTok and YouTube feed. The psychics would say he had genuine intentions but he was in a complicated situation. Remarkably, they accurately described him and even the other girls in his life. They would say that his ex was keeping an eye on me and that he would make our relationship official once everything ended with her. This was partially true, as his ex was shamelessly viewing my Instagram stories without hesitation, but he definitely had no plans to commit to me. These psychics kept my hopes alive by telling me what I wanted to hear. At the time, I perceived it as harmless. Afterall they were pretty accurate. Gradually, I became obsessed with seeking readings about various aspects of my life, hoping to gain insight into the future.

A psychic predicting our futures seems harmless, and many people don't even believe it's real. It is perceived as a lighthearted topic in culture. However, what people fail to understand is that psychics do not consult with God to obtain information about our future. It is important to remember that no one can approach the Father except through Christ. Tarot cards, crystals, and zodiac sign readings cannot bring us answers from God. So, if not from God, where do psychics get their information? The devil disguises himself as an angel of light. Although spirit guides, ancestors, and angels sound heavenly, it is the enemy in one of his many disguises. Psychics also operate under this phony light whether they are aware of it or not.

> But I am not surprised! Even Satan disguises himself as an angel of light. So it is no wonder that his servants also disguise themselves as servants of righteousness. In the end, they will receive the punishment their wicked deeds deserve.
>
> 1 Corinthians 11:14–15

Mr. Situationship's teammates encouraged him to make a move on me, but he was patient. He knew I was inexperienced, but simultaneously I was too scared I'd be a bad kisser anyways. It seemed like he was playing the slow game. When I confessed that I had never romantically talked to a guy before, he looked surprised, as if he didn't believe me **(red flag #2)**. At some point, he stopped asking to hang out, leaving me confused. Until one night, I received a Snapchat from him. Instead of seeing his face, I saw his girlfriend's **(red flag #3)**. Of course, I had to do my research and find her Instagram, to actually figure out that she indeed was his girlfriend. I assumed they had broken up, as he asked to hang out again once his ex had left. This time, the invitation went from "come over" to "let's go get ramen." I interpreted this as a sign that he was genuinely interested in pursuing me this time. (As I mentioned earlier, I was very naive.) We continued to spend time together for about two months, during which I developed genuine feelings for him. He gave me my first kiss, first cuddles, and my first experience of waking up next to someone. I laughed every time we kissed. Apparently, he found this immaturity on my part, but I have always been the one to laugh in every situation. I simply call it the joy of the Lord. His affection made me feel wanted for the first time.

One morning, after he had stayed the night, my mother called. Reluctant to answer because I didn't want her to know I had a boy in my dorm room, I eventually picked up the call. From the tone of her voice, I could tell it was bad news. "Michael passed away last night." My big cousin. He was so young. He lit up every room he walked into with his smile and boisterous laugh. He had been seeking a closer relationship with God and had started attending church, and I never got to say goodbye. I was left speechless. I left the dorm room because I didn't want to cry in front of Mr. Situationship. After breaking down in the bathroom, I returned and said, "My mom just told me that my cousin passed away." He, too, was speechless. Losing a loved one often leaves people unsure of what to say. I left once again to weep on the phone with my older sisters, and then returned once more. This time, I simply said, "It's a sad Sunday..." and found solace in his arms.

As we continued to spend time together, I sensed his desire for sex, but I had made a personal commitment to save my first time for my future husband. I struggled to communicate my boundaries verbally because I feared it might push him away, and I wasn't used to asserting myself. Although he never pressured me or made any explicit comments, things would get awkward when we found ourselves in intimate moments. I would abruptly pull away from his lips, kissing his forehead instead, then claiming exhaustion before falling asleep. During our hangouts, I'd show him J. Cole concerts on YouTube, and he introduced me to The Chappelle Show. I shared my record collection with him and even convinced him to smoke with me once.

Despite my decision to withhold physical intimacy, he would still do kind things like making waffles and getting breakfast on the mornings after our sleepovers. However, eventually, he began to catch on to my intentions and grew tired of the platonic nature of our sleepovers, cuddling, and movies with no sex. Either that, or he just had a type and I simply didn't fit the mold. Our last hangout together was before winter break, with a group of friends, when he took me aside into his dorm room for a conversation.

"Would you date me?" He asked, hypothetically.

I was taken aback by his willingness to address the "What are we?" topic, but because I genuinely liked him, I replied, "Yes, I would. I really like you." "Well, I'm not ready for a relationship," he responded. I couldn't help but wonder why he had initiated the conversation in the first place. The inner hopeless romantic in me couldn't resist sharing how I had caught feelings for him, but eventually, I mustered the strength to stand up and say, "Well... ima just going to go back to my dorm." The surprise on his face revealed that my reaction wasn't what he had anticipated. I don't know what was going through my head, but next thing you know I was venting to him about my friend drama, while giving him a back rub while Bas's entire album "Too High to Riot" played in the background. I wasn't sure when I would experience any form of affection again, so I got my final free sleepover, cuddling, and movie combo before leaving the next morning after breakfast. In my mind, I held onto hope that I would see him again after winter break, so I didn't fully process the end of our undefined relationship, but it was clear he had moved on.

A month after my cousin's passing, I received another phone call from my mother early in the morning. This time, I was alone, and I had a sense of what the call was about. "Papa G. passed away." My grandpa had been sick for years, frequently in and out of the hospital with countless prescriptions that only seemed to generate more health issues. He caught COVID-19 and couldn't take it. I had dreaded this day, but deep down, I knew it was inevitable. I broke down and wailed. Two deaths in the span of two months. Grandpa was the epitome of a grandfather. Every day, he would pick up my little sister and me from elementary school, surprising us with McDonald's happy meals. Funny enough, after we told him fast food was unhealthy, he upgraded us to Wendy's. He had built the backyard of my father's childhood home with his own two hands, where he planted his vegetable garden, played golf, constructed swing sets and trampolines for us, and taught us how to shoot a basketball. He had a knack for fixing anything—cars, cabinets, faucets, TVs, and computers. He taught us all 50 states, rewarding us with $10 to spend on candy. When we told him, "I love you," he would simply respond with an "Okay." Yet, his actions spoke volumes about his love for us.

During Winter Break, I attended two funerals, one for Michael from my mom's side of the family, and the other for Grandpa from my dad's side. Both occasions brought me to tears, and the music played during the services only intensified my emotions.

The song, "Closer" by Goapele will forever remind me of Michael, while "Ribbon in the Sky," by Stevie Wonder holds a special place in my heart for Grandpa.

It wouldn't have been a situationship if the two of us hadn't texted a couple of times during Winter Break. I even called him on Christmas, genuinely thinking that everything would return to normal once we were back on campus. However, my partner in crime decided to move back home to save money on dorms, which left me anticipating spending most of my time with Mr. Situationship and Judas. Interestingly, I noticed through social media that Judas and Mr. Situationship had become friends. Judas would post pictures of them on FaceTime, and they seemed quite close. Although I wasn't concerned about Judas having romantic intentions towards him, I couldn't help but feel a pang of jealousy towards their friendship. My worry intensified when I realized they had formed a friend group that included other girls who could potentially have romantic intentions.

I didn't want to lose everyone, but it seemed like they were all slipping away from me. My cousin, my grandpa, my partner in crime, my situationship, and my Judas. What I feared became a reality when we all returned to campus. I had planned to catch up with Judas and Mr. Situationship, but as I opened Snapchat to send a message, I came across Judas's private story. It was a video of a girl jumping into his arms. Deep down, I knew it was coming, but it still hurt immensely. It was the worst day I'd had at that point. I was grieving two family members, alone in my dorm room, missing my only friend, heartbroken over my first infatuation, and to top it off I was dealing with cramps (something I rarely experienced). I babied myself that day, clutching my heating pad, crying profusely, while indulging in sad music:

"Good Days" by SZA.

"FEEL" by Kendrick Lamar.

"Black Sheep" by Mick Jenkins.

Even though I felt betrayed, I couldn't help but search for answers, questioning why it wasn't me and whether my race, as a Black woman, played a role in his choice. Another thought crossed my mind: "He's going to need his hair twisted eventually." As it turned out, he ended up wearing his hair in an afro for the rest of the school year. While I wasn't too concerned about the romantic aspect not working out, I still desired to maintain a friendship. My heart has always been more significant than my brain in matters of relationships. Despite every friendship I've had eventually coming to an end or naturally growing distant over time, I often find myself reminiscing about every person who has been a part of my life. People may come and go, but I never forget anyone. Growing up with six siblings has taught me the value of relationships, and every person I meet holds a special place in my heart. I grieve every relationship that dies.

I felt kicked to the curb, even if it was unintentional. It was just unfortunate timing. Whenever I saw him, he would avoid eye contact, keep his head down, and go in the opposite direction. He even did the same thing when I saw him in the airport 6 months later, but it made me chuckle that time. The other universal language all D1 athletes speak is…silence.

Despite believing that he had no ill intentions, it still hurt that things didn't work out between us. In my mind, I had envisioned our relationship unfolding just like my big sister's. She attended the same school as I did, found a boyfriend who played basketball, and now, 11 years later, they are happily married with their first baby girl. Ever since I was 15, I have been praying that my first boyfriend would ultimately become my husband. Consequently, I am grateful that I never entered into a relationship with him. The idea of experiencing heartbreak multiple times before meeting "the one" doesn't fascinate me. I don't want so many people to have access to my heart. I don't wish to mourn over someone who is still alive but has chosen to walk out of my life. God just made me that way. Initially, I wanted us to remain friends, but I felt compelled to block him if I wanted to move forward. All he did was observe my stories, like my pictures, and ignore my presence in person. It drove me insane. As a result, I ended up creating my own playlist in an attempt to heal and move on.

"Smack a B****" by Rico Nasty.

"Land of the Snakes" by J.Cole.

"Damage" by H.E.R.

"Girl Like Me" by Jazmine Sullivan.

"Still Your Best" by Giveon.

God ended up convicting me delete one or two of these songs down the line, but they sure did comfort me in the moment.

WOUNDED

The weighty grief of everything I was going through overwhelmed me with anxiety. I even hesitated to step out of my dorm, fearing encounters with anyone on campus. Since Mr. Situationship was avoiding me I wasn't concerned with him, it was Judas. She had listened to me talk about how much I liked him all semester. I couldn't comprehend why she never at least warned me about his interest in her other friend. Every time I spotted her on campus, I deliberately ignored her, just as he did to me.

I fervently prayed to God, seeking resolution for these broken relationships day and night. One lonely night, I even prayed for a simple hug. Spending countless days in my dorm without uttering a word aloud, I could feel myself spiraling. Hoping that God would answer my prayer by sending Mr. Situationship, I left my dorm and headed to the Dining Commons, only to encounter Judas as I made my way out. I continued my usual practice of ignoring her, but this time she pursued me on her skateboard, "Jadaaaa! Jada?", she yelled. Finally catching up to me, she said "hey". Once she saw the distress on my face, she asked what was troubling me. Overwhelmed, I found myself falling into her arms, with tears streaming down my face. I felt immensely embarrassed. I attributed my tears to the recent deaths in my family, but deep down, I knew it was because of her. How could I communicate the pain she had caused me? I had never encountered a predicament like this with a friend before. Oh God, why would You lead me into the arms of my own Judas?

The first lesson God taught me on this journey was forgiveness. Forgiveness helps us more than it helps anyone else. Every day, I harbored anger, resentment, regret, and embarrassment in my heart. Yet, from my perspective, they were able to live emotionally carefree. It was detrimentally hindering my healing, meanwhile they continued their friendship as if nothing had happened. It wasn't fair that they could move on and live their lives without a second thought about my isolation and anguish. Back in high school, I had friends and teammates who would never dream of hurting my feelings or letting anyone harm me. They would be appalled if anyone dared to do so and would stand up for me. I was never one to engage in conflict, and I had never even needed to defend myself. Not saying it was healthy, but I embodied the essence of being unproblematic and nonconfrontational. All I could think was, "How could they do me like this?" My intentions were pure. I didn't deserve to endure such immense pain from the people I considered my friends. I suppose that's how the real world operates.

FACING FATE

It's one thing to face the consequences of our actions on Earth through our failures and mistakes, but it's important to remember that these consequences extend beyond this life alone. The Bible teaches us that the wages of sin is death, not only in this present life, but also in the afterlife. While we may experience loss of friends, jobs, money, opportunities, sanity, and peace here on Earth, we must recognize that in the spiritual realm, we risk our eternal life, which holds immeasurable value. This realization poses a fundamental question: Should I cease my current path and change my course in this life and the next, or should I persist in my current ways and continue?

It can be scary to acknowledge that we are innately prone to self-destruction. Some individuals attribute blame to the world, their parents, their circumstances, or even God. However, it requires personal accountability to truly understand our need for a Savior.

> People ruin their lives by their own foolishness and then are angry at the Lord.
>
> Proverbs 19:3 NLT

It is undeniably true that not everyone receives a favorable start on the right path in life, and even those who do may encounter unexpected challenges. Nevertheless, there comes a point where it becomes our individual responsibility to walk in righteousness. We must recognize that it is our own choices, when we veer away from God's ways, that lead us astray.

While some individuals may have more favorable circumstances, the odds are stacked against all of us, and each day we must consciously decide to make choices that lead to life instead of death. Embracing our own mortality is humbling, it's a hell of a reminder of the importance of our decisions and the impact they have on our eternal destiny.

CHAPTER FOUR

VOID.

VOID: an emptiness caused by the loss of something.

Sin leaves us with an empty void that only God can fill. Where we often go wrong is shoving various things into that whole, hoping they will save us, only to end up disappointed. This God shaped void, leads us into a never-ending cycle of bad habits, hopelessly chasing fulfillment.

SEARCHING FOR A SAVIOR

Many people are unaware that the desire for a savior resides within all of us, and it manifests in unexpected ways. We may try to escape our problems for a night through partying, hook-ups, or even indulging in a Netflix binge with a glass of wine, whilst unconsciously perceiving these activities as our saviors. It doesn't necessarily have to involve things the world considers "bad," such as alcoholism, drug addiction, or self-harm. It encompasses anything we turn to, seeking liberation from our circumstances. These are our "lowercase s" saviors. We yearn for something greater than ourselves, something that has it all figured out and possesses influence over us and our situations. Something about getting drunk in the club makes us feel like everything is okay but that happiness is temporary. Alcohol liberates us from our thoughts for a certain amount of time. It can take down the biggest, toughest man you know if he has enough beers. It has an influence on us that we can't control. There's something about retail therapy, a good meal, and a nice drink that relieves us, but it's temporary comfort. Immersing ourselves into a life we don't live and distracting ourselves with fictional drama on Netflix is not necessarily bigger than us, but it's outside of ourselves. We can't stand being alone with our thoughts because it forces us to examine reality. It can be overwhelming because we know we don't have all the answers.

When we run to these things, we often can't even see that deep down, we are searching for a true Savior. We hope that one day we'll finally run into something or someone that will actually save us from the world and its chaos.

> And what do you benefit if you gain the whole world but lose your own soul? Is anything worth more than your soul?
>
> **Matthew 16:26 NLT**

UNFULFILLED

This longing for a savior is our spirits crying out to us from within, shouting, "I need to be reconciled with God! Nothing you are doing can satisfy this hunger within me!" Truly, nothing we have done, chosen, or followed outside of God has ever saved us from ourselves. If we could prevent our own flesh from destroying our lives, we would not need God. The saviors in which we place our hope have no power. Even though they may offer temporary satisfaction or an escape, the problems we face remain, often growing even bigger. This is where we find ourselves trapped in destructive habits and cycles.

> Jesus replied, "Anyone who drinks this water will soon become thirsty again. But those who drink the water I give will never be thirsty again. It becomes a fresh, bubbling spring within them, giving them eternal life.
>
> John 4:13–14 NLT

During my battle with depression in High School, and even after attempting to ignore it, I experienced an insatiable hunger that nothing could appease. It left me unhappy in every circumstance, and it was exhausting. I even sought solace within the religion I had been taught, Christianity, but I remained unsatisfied because I had not developed a true connection with Christ. I tried church, but I did not try Jesus. What is religion worth without a genuine relationship? Can we truly believe in God if we simultaneously seek Him and the world's "answers"? I had a foundation in the Word of God, but I continued to search elsewhere. I even attempted to blend my prayers with manifestation and mix the Word of God with self-help. My faith was not solely in Him. It was in music, social media, weed, and everything else I continued to worship, including relationships. In my case, situationships.

Now when God made Adam and Eve. I don't think he envisioned the process of courtship to getting married within less than a year, changing into the "talking stage", situationship, relationship, engaged, then maybe married within 10+ years. Our generation is plagued by toxicity, with a significant lack of love and respect towards one another. We are not gentle with each other's feelings, and many people have their guard up due to the fear of getting hurt. However, deep down inside, everyone longs for something real. The challenges we face in relationships today are numerous, and I believe it's because the devil is intimidated by the power of love. Therefore, he concentrates on perverting its purity. He knows that the Bible repeatedly emphasizes the strength of love and uses it against us, causing hurt and leading people to hurt each other. Hurt people hurt people, and the devil hardens hearts, leaving many in disbelief that true love exists. Perhaps this is why it's so difficult for some of us to believe in a loving Heavenly Father.

I grew up surrounded by examples of healthy, long-lasting marriages and relationships. However, whenever I scrolled through social media or went to school, I would fear that I would end up alone. Society convinced me that black women like me, with short 4c hair standing at the height of 5 feet and 10 inches, were deemed unlovable. Even though I humbly found myself absolutely gorgeous and multi-faceted, I never seemed to capture the attention of the guys I liked. And if I did, I couldn't maintain their interest. I have always genuinely desired a healthy love, and toxic behavior has never been a part of me. My heart has always been fragile, and knowing that I don't handle heartbreak well, I couldn't allow myself to be naive. I still have that same fragile heart, but it's no longer easily accessible because I have set up non-negotiables and boundaries. If I was walking with God, His wisdom would have protected me from those feelings of abandonment. He does so now, and even though I experience moments of loneliness, I know He's safeguarding my heart.

Guarding our hearts doesn't mean being emotionally unavailable. It means setting healthy boundaries, having reasonable non-negotiables, and fostering mutual respect. It's important to expect at least the bare minimum, and if it's not offered, it's time to move on. While I don't believe that God chooses our spouses from birth, He has provided us with everything we need to know when desiring a loving relationship. He instructs us to wait until marriage because sex is the act of two individuals becoming one flesh—a bond meant to last a lifetime. It produces offspring, which is also meant to last a lifetime. When that bond is shared with multiple people, it leaves our souls yearning for that lifelong connection. And when that person isn't there, it hurts. God clearly defines what love is, yet we continue to seek it from people who have distorted God's love into something poisonous and addictive.

> Love is patient and kind. Love is not jealous or boastful or proud or rude. It does not demand its own way. It is not irritable, and it keeps no record of being wronged. It does not rejoice about injustice but rejoices whenever the truth wins out. Love never gives up, never loses faith, is always hopeful, and endures through every circumstance. Prophecy and speaking in unknown languages and special knowledge will become useless. But love will last forever!
>
> 1 Corinthians 13:4–8

Love eradicates trust issues and prevents emotional or physical abuse. It fosters encouragement without any intention of competition or comparison. Love doesn't place the other person above everything else; rather, it involves being each other's cheerleaders while maintaining humility.

Love is a haven where kindness prevails, even when the world fails to offer it. It strikes a balance between giving and receiving, and it prioritizes the needs of the other person. Love involves doing things that bring joy to the other person, even if we don't personally find enjoyment in them. It is willing to try new experiences to please the other, while remaining true to our own character. Love is considerate of the other person's feelings and desires, and it readily forgives when a genuine apology is given. It does not hold grudges or resort to blackmail. Love creates a home where we can let our guards down, without bitterness or irritability that may arise in us with the world.

Love doesn't initiate petty arguments for amusement, nor does it care about who is right or wrong. The ultimate goal is to win together, even if it requires compromise. This kind of love requires selflessness and genuinely considers the other person's point of view.

Love doesn't abandon the relationship during challenging times; instead, it prays and works towards better days. By "rough patches," I refer to difficulties such as financial issues, depression, or family struggles—situations that life throws at everyone. Love never loses faith in the strength of the bond shared between two individuals and maintains hope for better times when faced with trouble.

When we entertain toxic love in our lives, we inadvertently endorse the manipulation of this pure love I speak of. It's essential to recognize that real love exists. There is no need to cling to toxic or minimal relationships out of fear that there might be nothing more. In the Kingdom of God, there is no shortage of healthy love available, provided we are willing to exemplify this genuine love ourselves. If we feel unfamiliar with this kind of love or struggle to recognize it, let this serve as a reminder that God Himself is the greatest teacher of love. When we earnestly seek it, He will reveal it to us. I wish someone had shared this wisdom with me earlier.

Relationships are the closest thing we have to a savior in this world. They reflect the model of what our relationship with God should be like. Healthy relationships are beneficial, allowing us to confide in others and find comfort. The Bible even says that it is not good for man to be alone. However, people can be unreliable, leaving us unfulfilled at times, much like our other "saviors".

Interestingly, when I listen to love songs, I find myself looking towards the sky as if I were singing to God. He is my first love after all. For example, listening to the lyrics of songs like "CPR" by Summer Walker always resonate with the intimacy I share with Him and the dependence I place on Him. God deliberately orchestrated this connection. He refers to us as His bride, and Jesus as our groom. Our relationship with Him, as the church, is akin to a marriage. Marriage, as we all know, is founded on love and devotion, and that is precisely what we should offer to God.

It truly bewilders me how people find it peculiar to praise God in such a manner, yet they never question it when others worship their partners in the same way. I've listened to love songs, contemplating different boys who broke my heart, leaving me feeling helpless. I've even found myself doing the same thing with my friends. It's become a habit of mine to place people on a pedestal, investing so much of myself in them, only to be left unfulfilled. When we place our faith solely in people, we are bound to stumble. People are imperfect and they too need God. How can our savior be someone who also requires a Savior? When they stumble, will they be able to save us? Moreover, will we be okay with them no longer being the savior they once were when they undergo change? The Lord understands that one of our initial instincts is to replace Him with a person, and He warns us because He knows the nature of a human is unreliable and incapable of sustaining one another alone.

It is better to take refuge in the Lord than to trust in people.

Psalms 118:8 NLT

DIVISION

> No one can serve two masters; for either he will hate the one and love the other, or he will be devoted to the one and despise the other. You cannot serve God and mammon [money, possessions, fame, status, or whatever is valued more than the Lord].
>
> Matthew 6:24 AMP

We understand that sin is what creates a separation between us and God, but have you ever wondered how exactly sin separates us from Him? Let's consider this scenario: Imagine being in a long-term, healthy relationship, and suddenly your partner starts engaging in cheating, lying, and growing distant. They text other romantic interests while sitting right next to you, spend nights away without explanation, and when they are with you, they lack affection. It begins to feel as though they don't truly care for you, despite their words of "I love you." Clearly, their actions contradict their verbal expressions. It becomes evident that they cannot genuinely love you while actively disrespecting and denying you on a daily basis. Naturally, you start feeling hurt, and this creates division within your once-healthy relationship. They attempted to please both you and others simultaneously, but in doing so, they ended up loving the other person while neglecting and hating you.

In the same way, our relationship with God can also experience division. When there is a division in our relationship with Him, it is akin to cheating on Him. The consequences, however, are much higher than in a romantic relationship. They extend beyond this life and have eternal implications. By indulging in a sinful lifestyle and repeatedly choosing our own desires over God's will, we become desensitized to His love for us. Sin becomes the weapon that drives a wedge between us and God, turning us into His enemies. Being an enemy means actively opposing or being hostile towards someone or something. Every sin, whether it be pride or murder, has the same effect of creating division between us and God.

To truly grasp the significance of sin's impact, we need to recognize the weight it carries in our relationship with our Creator. It is a serious matter that jeopardizes our eternal destiny. However, there is hope. God, in His great love for us, provided a solution to bridge the gap caused by sin. Through the sacrifice of Jesus Christ on the cross, we have the opportunity to be reconciled with God and restored to a harmonious relationship with Him. It is through repentance and faith in Jesus that we can experience forgiveness and the removal of sin's power in our lives.

> You adulterers! Don't you realize that friendship with the world makes you an enemy of God? I say it again: If you want to be a friend of the world, you make yourself an enemy of God.
>
> James 4:4 NLT

Usually, when someone cheats in a relationship, that person is abandoned by the other. Perhaps they even face the wrath of their partner, with their car set on fire and all their belongings thrown inside. It's important to remember that God is not like man; He is faithful, and His reaction is not to seek revenge for how we have hurt Him. After true repentance, He does not abandon us. However, this division creates an illusion in our minds that God is mad at us and that He won't accept us, because that is the reaction we would usually expect from a human. Even so, it is the reaction we would have ourselves if someone treated us the way we have treated God. It becomes difficult to believe that He is waiting for us on the other side, and all we have to do is run to Him. Fortunately, He accepts us with open arms when we return, but He's not going to chase after us if we continuously hide from Him. He never forces Himself. He wants us to chase after Him in the same way we chase after sin. Many people see the division and hold themselves back because they feel they must clean up their lives before they come to Him. We sit and see the sin, the chaos, and the dirt, and we want to hide from Him. We feel unworthy of approaching Him. This division keeps us stagnant. We pace back and forth against the wall that separates us from Him, contemplating what we'll do, what we'll say, and how things will change, as if He hasn't been watching us the entire time. God is not intimidated by division like we are, and He will not embarrass us. There is nothing to be afraid of. In relationships, we cannot seek reconciliation with the other person without physically going to them. Therefore, sitting in division before coming to God will not result in any progress because the messes we have made cannot be cleaned up without Him. I've done the same thing to my parents after an argument or a mistake, and the whole time, they were just sitting with open arms, waiting for me to run back with sincere remorse because they love like God.

PART II

SERVING GOD.

CHAPTER FIVE

DEATH.

In the same way, there is joy in the presence of God's angels when even one sinner repents.

Luke 15:10 NLT

My first semester of college chewed me up and spit me out. I was left feeling worn out and defeated. There were two factors at play: the enemy taking advantage of my naivety, and the trials of life itself. Sometimes, "ish" happens. The devil tempted me with the allure of the "college experience." He promised that these new friends would be good for me, but instead, they caused me pain. He assured me that I'd be loved by this guy, yet he treated me as if I didn't exist. He suggested that getting high or drunk, or both, would take away my pain, but in reality, it only provided temporary numbness. He even convinced me that tarot card readings would bring me peace, but instead, they put me in the presence of demons that I had to fight later. Lastly, he persuaded me that following the crowd was the path to walk on, but it only left me heartbroken and facing academic probation. Within just one semester, I became unrecognizable. The enemy didn't care about my well-being, peace, healing, relationships, education, or anything else. His sole objective was to kill my spirit, steal my joy, and destroy my life. He was cunning and deceitful. I thought we were merely having a good time, but he left me burdened with guilt, shame, condemnation, an immense void in my heart that only Jesus could fill, and a gigantic mess of a life that could only be restored by God.

When I realized that I was on my own and that none of my friends were coming to rescue me, I placed my complete faith in God. After all, who else could I turn to?

In most cases, death is a dreaded event. However, with God, it is a moment that is actually celebrated by angels because it signifies a rebirth. In fact, we are called to experience a daily death—the death of our flesh.

Most people I know have dedicated their lives to Christ within the physical confines of a church, surrounded by loved ones. However, my experience was slightly different. It showed me that discovering a relationship with God is not confined to a church building; it is simply found in Christ. Jesus said, "Come to me, all who are weary." And although the following are great vessels, He did not even say "Come to church all who are weary", or "Come to your Christian friends or pastors all who are weary". He simply invites us to come to Him. People often forget that God is omnipresent, and when we accept Him, our bodies become literal temples of the Holy Spirit. This realization taught me the true meaning of having a relationship with God. In the past, religion held no real significance in my life. Merely attending church every Sunday was not enough to save my soul, but it did serve as a lifeline when I needed it most. It was an unexpected tool that helped me later on—a means of escape.

> **Direct your children onto the right path, and when they are older, they will not leave it.**
>
> **Proverbs 22:6 NLT**

My introduction to Christ began with my Grandmother. She taught my little sister and me The Lord's Prayer and Psalm 23 every night we slept over at her house until we knew them by heart. She also took us to Sunday School every week. Although I didn't particularly enjoy her church, the one my parents attended felt like home. Going with my Grandma meant being the only black child in a giant sea of white people in my suburban, Republican hometown. It meant encountering familiar faces from elementary school, which didn't bother me, but her church was vast, impersonal, and lacked a sense of community. Nevertheless, it did have a visually pleasing exterior, and I still catch sight of it every time I drive back home. It's the same size as my entire neighborhood. However, credit must be given where it is due. That church had the best summer camp I ever attended. Camping in a tent in San Clemente, CA, with my closest friends, sitting around a bonfire roasting marshmallows, and experiencing the unique joy of swimming in the ocean while it rained—it was the most adventurous thing I had ever done. Although I can't recall what I learned about Jesus during that time, it remains a cherished memory.

Attending church with my parents gave me the option to join either the children's service or the adult service. I was born into this church family. It meant receiving endless hugs and kisses from the congregation, along with complimentary peppermints, butterscotches, and strawberry candies from the nice old ladies. It meant being moved by the beautiful live worship music, with tears streaming down the faces of everyone present. Every Sunday I watched my 6'2" mother, raise her hands toward the sky during worship with her heels making her so much taller, I wondered if she'd actually reach God's hands someday. It meant being served sweet cranberry juice and small crackers on shiny gold platters, which only made me hungrier and increased my excitement to persuade my dad to let us get donuts after the service. And it meant receiving a warm hug from our big and tall pastor with the kindest smile every Sunday, after laughing at all his Bible jokes during the sermon. Apparently, when I was born, he provided me with an ample supply of baby formula, diapers, clothes, and anything else a baby might need. I had no idea of what was happening during those services. I simply couldn't wait for the part where I could finally sit down after worship, as my legs grew tired, and begin a game of Tic Tac Toe on the offering envelope with my sisters.

Going to this church on the right Sunday also meant seeing girls who resembled older versions of me gracefully moving down the aisles in gold and white drapes, adorned with purple ribbons that created beautiful swirls in the air. It was praise dance, and I longed to be just like them. My father raised my four sisters and me as basketball players, so I was hesitant to ask if I could join. When my mom introduced the idea of joining a cheerleading team, he made a funny remark, leaving me unsure of how he would react to something like praise dance. Despite my uncertainties, we joined the dance group, and during the only performance I remember, my father sat in the front row with a tight-lipped smile and shiny red cheekbones, trying to hold back tears while he recorded on his android. He always makes the same face when he's holding back happy tears. Swirling my ribbon in the air, I felt so beautiful. However, during rehearsals, I felt insecure as I realized I was the only one struggling with a proper ballet leap. Though I don't know how it appeared to others, I felt like I was flying just like the other girls. Unfortunately, my dance teacher's chuckle whenever it was my turn indicated otherwise. A leap wasn't as easy as a layup.

I didn't particularly enjoy Sunday School at that church because I struggled to make friends with most of the other Black kids. For some reason I still struggle to make friends at church, but now it actually bothers me. As always, I clung to my little sister. This church also had a church camp, but it wasn't as enjoyable as the other one. However, that was alright.

We didn't spend the nights at this church camp. It may not have been as funded or as fun, but this was the first time that I made the decision to give my life to Christ. The pastor's daughter did her best to teach us about Jesus, in a way that a child could understand. As far as I could comprehend at that time, I truly desired to place my life in His hands. But being shy, I chose to remain seated next to my little sister when she called us to the altar. I lowered my head and whispered the prayer to myself, "Jesus, I'm too shy to go up there, but I want my life to be in your hands." From that moment onward, every time the pastor made an altar call, I silently repeated the prayer of salvation to myself. I wasn't sure if Jesus heard me, but I wanted to ensure that if I were to die, I would go to heaven. Now, I understand that it's not necessary to repeat the prayer of salvation every time we make mistakes; God simply calls us to repent because He knows we will stumble.

So yes, I was raised in the church. No, I am not a victim of being raised in a cult, although I acknowledge that such cults do exist. They are just one of the many disguises the devil uses to divert people from the truth. Unfortunately, the Bible has been misused to justify slavery, abuse, hypocrisy, hatred, misogyny, racism, and other forms of injustice. Naturally, nobody wants to be associated with that. However, the wrongdoings of those who manipulate the Word have nothing to do with who God truly is. <u>We must be able to</u>

<u>separate the bad experiences we've had with people who call themselves Christians, from who Christ truly is.</u> The devil is cunning, like a slick serpent, and he too has followers. He distorts the truth, making it appear evil, so that you and I won't believe in it. He may even be doing it within your church at this very moment. Alternatively, he may be camouflaging the darkness within something you believe in, making it appear heavenly.

One book, the Holy Bible, has been divided into several different religions and denominations. Personally, I don't consider myself religious. Religion, organized by man based on their interpretation of what a relationship with God should look like, is something that Jesus didn't particularly favor. He referred to the legalistic religious leaders, the Pharisees, as hypocrites. To be honest, I'm not even fond of using the term "Christian." I only use it because it's commonly understood to mean "a person who believes in Jesus." In the Bible, the term "Christian" is used sparingly. I prefer to call myself a Believer, which is short for someone who believes in the Father, the Son, and the Holy Spirit. I believe that the Father sent His Son to die for my sins and that He left His Spirit with me so that I could have the opportunity for eternal life with Him. Alternatively, I might describe myself as a non-denominational Christian. In the eyes of others, I may not appear any different from the "religious." Some might even label me as a Jesus freak or a Bible thumper, but I am proud and unashamed, and I don't care that those terms are derogatory. At the same time some religious people may see me as a fraud, just as the Pharisees believed Jesus was a fraud, and just as the prophets were persecuted by the religious leaders. We'd be foolish not to expect the same to happen to us. But my purpose is not to please man but to please God.

My goal here is not to reinforce the world's stereotype of Christianity. I am simply tired of seeing Him being misunderstood and redefined by the world due to the misrepresentation of Him, and because those who truly know Him fail to advocate for Him. Jesus wasn't someone who wore a suit and tie every Sunday on a grand stage, hiding behind hypocrisy and asking for money. He was building meaningful relationships with anyone willing to listen, healing those who believed in His power to heal, and preparing His disciples to do the same. My intention is to encourage you to stop relying on the world to define who God is and instead get to know Him for yourself through the Scriptures and by finding a genuine community of Believers. I want you to see the God I see because I'm beginning to realize that everyone has their own god, whether they identify as Christian or not, and these "gods" are nothing more than powerless lower-case "g"s. Big G is sovereign.

So far, every significant encounter I've had with Christ has occurred in solitude, apart from a few moments shared with my sister or during prayer calls. I rededicated my life to Christ in January of 2021 while in my freshman year dorm room, which felt like a jail cell, as I was watching a sermon by Michael Todd in the Forgiveness University (FU) series, attempting to recover from heartbreak and betrayal. This was the moment when I reconciled with our Heavenly Father and denounced my flesh as my ruler. My moment of repentance was marked by me kneeling with my head bowed to the ground, weeping for forgiveness, overwhelmed by pain, and finally acknowledging my weakness and desperate need for a "big S" Savior. It was the first time I felt His loving arms wrapped around me, providing comfort to my spirit. Suddenly, the warmth of the sun shining on my face felt like a gentle kiss from heaven. I didn't anticipate any supernatural experiences following that moment, but after engaging in intense spiritual warfare that involved seeing my own demons, I actually heard His voice.

For several days, I kept hearing my name whispered in soft, faint tones, as if someone were leaning over my shoulder and speaking directly into my ear. At first, I didn't think much of it because, by that point, after seeing evil spirits, I questioned my own sanity. I shared this with my sister, who was discipling me at the time, and she directed me to read 1 Samuel 3.

One night Eli, who was almost blind by now, had gone to bed. Suddenly the Lord called out, "Samuel!" "Yes?" Samuel replied. "What is it?" He got up and ran to Eli. "Here I am. Did you call me?" "I didn't call you," Eli replied. "Go back to bed." So he did. Then the Lord called out again, "Samuel!" Again Samuel got up and went to Eli. "Here I am. Did you call me?" "I didn't call you, my son," Eli said. "Go back to bed." Samuel did not yet know the Lord because he had never had a message from the Lord before. So the Lord called a third time, and once more Samuel got up and went to Eli. "Here I am. Did you call me?" Then Eli realized it was the Lord who was calling the boy. So he said to Samuel, "Go and lie down again, and if someone calls again, say, 'Speak, Lord , your servant is listening.'" So Samuel went back to bed. And the Lord came and called as before, "Samuel! Samuel!" And Samuel replied, "Speak, your servant is listening."

1 Samuel 3:2,4–10 NLT

She instructed me to lie down that night and give God my

listening ear, so that's exactly what I did, albeit with some fear. In the Bible, we often witness men experiencing fear when approached by angels, and that was my exact reaction. I lay down while on the phone with my older sister, who guided me through the process. She suggested that I end the call, but I was hesitant to do so. While she found my fear amusing, it was genuinely real to me. As soon as I ended the call, I started playing worship music to calm myself down and said, "God I'm listening".

I pondered whether I could truly consider myself as actively listening if I was also listening to worship music simultaneously. After all, the voice of God is often described as still and small. If I genuinely wanted to hear Him, I needed to tune out all other distractions. Thus, I turned off the music. However, even after turning it off, I continued to hear music. I double-checked my phone to ensure there was no music playing, which was indeed the case. This situation instilled even more fear within me. I began questioning my sanity. The music I heard was celestial in nature, resembling an intensified version of YouTube meditation worship music. I felt an ethereal lightness within my body, as though I were floating, despite still lying on my back. Then, a soft voice began singing in my ears, creating an effect similar to wearing headphones. Unfortunately, my fear disrupted the experience, preventing me from calmly embracing the moment. Laughably, my Gen-Z instincts led me to call my sister back in the midst of it. Trembling, I uttered, "Um... I'm hearing things." My sister found my fear highly amusing. "Jada, relax... What do you hear?" she asked.

"I don't know, but it sounds so beautiful," I replied.

All she could do was laugh at my expense. Eventually, the music, singing, and floating sensation subsided. I proceeded to explain the situation to her, and we concluded that God's angels were rejoicing at my return home. Nevertheless, fear still lingered within me. My sister remained on the phone with me throughout the night until I drifted off to sleep.

The next day, I awoke with heightened senses. Every little noise startled me, from the rustling of the wind in the trees to passing cars and conversations outside. Since nobody else was home, I resorted to my usual routine during such moments. I switched on the large flat-screen TV to play music videos and immersed myself in a personal at-home concert, releasing my heartbreak and grief while listening to Giveon and Jazmine Sullivan songs. I contacted my sister, and she advised me to listen for God's voice again, without seeking her guidance. I settled onto the couch and turned off the music. In silence, I took a moment to pray as the sunlight streamed through the windows, gently warming my face. Once more, I uttered, "God, I'm listening." Then, in a still, small voice, I heard, "God is working in you. God is working on you."

For God is working in you, giving you the desire and the power to do what pleases him.

Philippians 2:13 NLT

RECONCILIATION

> Not only is this so, but we also boast in God through our Lord Jesus Christ, through whom we have now received reconciliation.
>
> Romans 5:11 NIV

As I reflect on that time, I am in awe. Despite my being overwhelmed and trembling fear that made me beg God to speak to me in less scary ways moving forward, I am amazed. Did He really think of me? The omnipresent creator of the universe and everything in it took the time to acknowledge me? Even though I had disobeyed, doubted, and completely abandoned Him, He was glad to see me? And not only that, He is actively working within me? Why did He choose to rescue me from the world at that moment? I felt like the Samaritan woman at the well. Jesus was on His way to Galilee but intentionally went out of His way, through Samaria, to speak to her. This woman had been rejected and shunned by society. Yet, He thought of her and purposely met her. That's exactly what He did for me. I was heading towards destruction, but He took a detour and found me.

He truly leaves the 99. He cares about my heartbreak, the pain that others grew tired of hearing about, and the times when I simply need a hug. His care is so immense that He never belittles my pain, even though He surely has other important matters to attend to. Moreover, as He merely consoles me, He is also saving lives, providing for His children, commanding the Sun and Moon to rise and fall, and sending His angels to protect us. All with ease.

The human mind cannot fathom His love or grasp His works. My own testimonies and the testimonies of others leave me speechless. What more can I say but "My God!"? What else can I do but praise Him? Whenever doubts arise, I only need to remind myself of what He has done. He saved me from her. He saved me from myself.

> So you have not received a spirit that makes you fearful slaves. Instead, you received God's Spirit when he adopted you as his own children. Now we call him, 'Abba, Father.' For his Spirit joins with our spirit to affirm that we are God's children.
>
> Romans 8:15–16 NLT

Now we call Him Abba, Father. Regardless of our age or wisdom, we have become His beloved children. A good father is loyal and he loves, corrects, advises, counsels, and teaches his child. As children, we humbly take our place as students of life, with a moldable mind, open to listening, receiving, and being mentored. Returning to being His child doesn't mean regressing into immaturity or foolishness; rather, it means recognizing and respecting His authority over our lives. Reconciliation relieves us from the burden of worry and the constant need for all the answers. Now we can rest in our Father's shelter and remain embraced by Him. He grants us a peace that surpasses all understanding and unexplainable joy amidst difficulties.

God's love keeps no record of wrongs. No matter how

embarrassed or ashamed we may feel at times, God's love reminds us that we have no reason to feel that way. For some of us, it may take longer to realize that we need supernatural guidance, and unfortunately, some may never get there. However, no matter how long it takes, He patiently waits for us. Every single soul matters deeply in His heart.

> Dear Heavenly Father,
>
> I come to you from the depths of my heart. I realize that I am a sinner, and I come to repent and ask for forgiveness of my sins. I believe that Jesus is the Son of God and that He died for my sins and rose from the dead on the third day. I believe in the Father, The Son, and The Holy Spirit. I turn away from my sins and ask that you come into my heart and life. I will trust and follow you as my Lord and Savior. I confess with my mouth that I am saved by the blood of Jesus, and You are now my Lord and Savior.
>
> In Jesus name,
> AMEN.

Saying this prayer demonstrates our faith in God for salvation, but faith alone is not enough. It must be accompanied by action. Repentance involves expressing sincere remorse for our sins and making a deliberate choice to turn away from them. To illustrate, imagine if your partner apologized for hurting you but continued to cheat. Likewise, how do you think God feels when people say the "sinner's prayer" or the "prayer of repentance" but fail to follow through with their actions?

IDENTIFYING THE FLESH

In order to depart from sin, repent, and truly die to ourselves daily, it's important we identify our flesh so that we are aware of what God doesn't approve of. For instance:

What areas of my life are in rebellion against God?

What is inside of me that is pursuing death?

Who was I?

> For the sinful nature is always hostile to God. It never did obey God's laws, and it never will. That's why those who are still under the control of their sinful nature can never please God.
>
> Romans 8:7–8 NLT

Understanding this verse makes it easy to identify the flesh. Every desire within us that contradicts the word of God is the flesh. Everything within us that is hostile towards anything having to do with God, and every intrusive urge, that we usually would obey, that puts us right back into the shackles of our flesh.

When I identified my own sinful nature, it was disheartening to discover that most of me needed to die. Especially since the world had given those things their stamp of approval. While behaviors like wild parties, smoking weed, immodesty, and lust may have been shamed 80 years ago, they are now rather praised. It is now a societal norm to watch pornography, send explicit images, get heavily intoxicated every weekend, and engage in casual sexual relationships. So of course, in my eyes and in the eyes of others, I was a saint. During my first year of college, people considered me a "sweetheart" when they discovered I was a virgin who had never been in a relationship, never tried drugs or alcohol, and hadn't even had my first kiss. Even after I became a pothead, got crossfaded at parties, and had my first kiss, people still saw me as "sweet and innocent Jada." However, this was a dangerous territory to walk in, because if God had ended my life prematurely and I hadn't had a chance to repent, on Judgment Day He would not have referred to me as His sweetheart like everyone else did. He would have said, "Depart from me, I never knew you." People may judge us by their standard, but they are not in control of our fate. On judgement day, it is not my beloved friends who will deem me worthy of heaven or hell, it will be God. If God judged based on societal standards that accept everything as good and true, we would all go to Heaven. Our perception of our own goodness is irrelevant. I was surprised to discover that God wasn't necessarily pleased with every aspect of my character, even though people had always considered me a "good person." While He acknowledged the kind and sweet parts of me, He also saw areas that needed to be transformed. Most people define a "bad person" based on their actions, but God is not intimidated by our mistakes and negative habits. He saw my sinful nature, recognized the need for it to be eradicated, and began cultivating a new creation within me. We often take it personally when others recognize our shortcomings and attempt to make us better. However, we should abandon the ideology that we are perfect the way we are and that people should learn how to deal with us. We've all got some growth to do, and God is with us through it.

BURYING THE FLESH

> We know that our old sinful selves were crucified with Christ so that sin might lose its power in our lives. We are no longer slaves to sin. For when we died with Christ we were set free from the power of sin.
>
> Romans 6:6–7 NLT

Dearly Beloved,

We are gathered here today to mourn the passing of my flesh. Her death signifies my rebirth. She was a wild one, holding complete control over me for the first 18 years of my life. She caused me immense depression and anxiety, almost convincing me that I could comfortably continue as her slave. As she dies, the relationships she formed will wither away with her, and we mourn the loss of companionship as we tread this narrow path. The memories she created now stain my mind, a constant reminder that ignorance brings bliss while knowledge burdens. With her demise, the destructive habits she introduced me to have also perished. Although she still tries to lure me back to my old ways from her grave, her power is limited. She has been crucified with Christ, and what once brought pleasure now brings agony. I will never forget her determination to keep company and loyalty to our betrayers. She lacked self-respect and let people walk all over me. She sought approval from people who followed dangerous standards and led me down a treacherous path. She was the kind of person who gained your trust only to betray you. She means nothing to me. Her intentions were always evil. It's because of her that I now must break the addictive habits she instilled in me. She continues to haunt me daily, her cries echoing from her grave, attempting to manipulate me once again. She may be gone, but unfortunately, she will always be with us. Goodbye old friends, goodbye old habits, and fare-frickin-well my flesh.

The best way I can describe burying the flesh is by likening it to Leonardo DiCaprio's character in The Basketball Diaries during his heroin withdrawals. After becoming addicted to the world and its offerings, it becomes a drug. Of course actual drugs do this, but so does toxic love, empty companionship, and bad habits. Although embracing Christ was a significant moment, I felt a sense of mourning. I mourned the loss of friends, moments, and the sinful life I lived. It wouldn't be called "dying to self" if it weren't painful. It means choosing one part of ourselves over the other, and even though it's the right choice, it hurts. We can't have it both ways. In the beginning, dying to self daily feels like mourning the things we can no longer indulge in when faced with temptation, mourning the company we can no longer keep when they invite us out, and mourning the blissful ignorance we once lived in. I deliberately use the word "mourning." I have never experienced such emotional pain as I have during this time in my life. It's akin to spiritual withdrawal. However, every time we choose to die to self, it brings a victorious feeling knowing that we won't be facing its consequences. And although temptations don't magically vanish, it becomes easier to die to self with each passing day.

> The temptations in your life are no different from what others experience. And God is faithful. He will not allow the temptation to be more than you can stand. When you are tempted, he will show you a way out so that you can endure.
>
> 1 Corinthians 10:13 NLT

CHAPTER SIX

THE LIFTED VEIL.

> But whenever someone turns to the Lord, the veil is taken away. For the Lord is the Spirit, and wherever the Spirit of the Lord is, there is freedom. So all of us who have had that veil removed can see and reflect the glory of the Lord. And the Lord—who is the Spirit—makes us more and more like him as we are changed into his glorious image.
>
> 2 Corinthians 3:16–18 NLT

The veil that clouded my understanding was finally lifted, revealing the truth about my actions. Quitting smoking weed, giving up tarot readings, or abstaining from pornography were not things I desired. I had no concept of controlling my flesh. I don't think I would have comprehended the **darkness** and **deception** behind my sin, if I had instantly become perfect after committing my life to Christ. I was put to the test: who would I truly serve? Although I declared my devotion to Christ, would my actions align with my confession?

One morning, as I prepared to watch pornography as I usually did, the Holy Spirit intervened. He prompted me to turn away from everything my flesh desired. That day, I went cold turkey on porn, but I still had the inclination to indulge in smoking weed and watching tarot readings. So I continued satisfying those cravings. It wasn't until God revealed to me the spiritual reality of my sin that I finally ceased those habits.

TEST 1: TAROT READINGS

Initially, I had planned to never watch another tarot reading. However, I couldn't resist when my favorite psychics released new videos. The process involved picking crystals or cards, and they would interpret the situation in various areas of my life. It felt entertaining, and I developed a sense of connection with these readers through the screen. After all, they seemed to know everything about me. At times, I even felt desperate enough to consider reaching out to them for more information. That year, I met a classmate who also dabbled in tarot card readings. Whenever she mentioned it, I would ask her for a reading, but she never followed through. One day, while discussing my situationship over the phone with her, she finally offered to give me a reading. Excitedly, I accepted. Ironically, this offer finally came after I had made the decision to follow Jesus. She promised to call me back after the reading and ended the conversation. In that moment, I sat in silence, overwhelmed by immediate regret. Although I knew it was wrong, I was still weak, succumbing to the desires of my flesh. I continued to blindly follow my own desires. My classmate eventually called back and shared information I was already aware of regarding my situation. I had hoped she would say that he would return, but instead, she revealed that he had been playing games all along. It was disheartening.

Shortly after that incident, I began experiencing things in the spiritual realm that were beyond my imagination. The veil had been lifted, and I finally saw what happened every time I got these readings. As I went to sleep, I would see dark figures resembling the grim reaper lurking by my bed and in my doorway. At the time, my older sister was mentoring me, and I described these experiences as "feeling darkness." I would sit on my bed every night overcome by fear and anxiety, and the intensity would only escalate. I recall leaving my dorm room at 3:00am one night because I believed that I would die if I stayed. It was a raw, bone-chilling fear—like something out of a horror movie. Is this what rappers mean when they mention fighting demons? Only when I left the room did I experience peace, but upon returning, the anxiety would consume me once again. I resorted to playing worship music while I slept, but it only helped me get through the night. I needed assistance, but the shame prevented me from confiding in anyone. It was embarrassing to admit that I had been obsessed with tarot readings for so long, simply because I was a hopeless romantic. I failed to realize that it was the devil trying to keep me silent, for true freedom lay beyond my confession.

> Confess your sins to each other and pray for each other so that you may be healed. The earnest prayer of a righteous person has great power and produces wonderful results.
>
> James 5:16 NLT

I had been speaking to my sister on the phone every day during this period, as she was discipling me in my spiritual journey. During one of our conversations, I finally opened up and confessed. I knew it was necessary. Initially, I had claimed that I only watched tarot readings on TikTok, then I admitted to watching a few on YouTube, and eventually I told her that I had received an actual tarot reading in real life. Her reaction heightened my fear. She said, "Hold on, I need to call my sister and ask her to pray because I'm not sure if I'm equipped to handle this spiritually." I was sitting there like, "whatchumean?! Is it that serious?" She reached out to her sister in Christ, I confessed once again, and they prayed over me with great power and authority. I was sobbing, and as I cried, I felt a sense of release. I was overwhelmed with regret and shame, but I was liberated.

> Whatever you have said in the dark will be heard in the light, and what you have whispered behind closed doors will be shouted from the housetops for all to hear!
>
> Luke 12:3 NLT

Was it possible that I had just been delivered from demonic oppression over the phone? After I had given my life to Christ while watching YouTube? After the prayer, I stayed on the phone with my sister throughout the night. She taught me how to pray over my room whenever I felt afraid. She advised me to confront the situation directly instead of avoiding it. So there I was in my dorm, shouting "Blood of Jesus!" and, "I cast out the spirit of the devil in the name of Jesus!" I'm sure my floormates were puzzled by the sound of worship music, sermons, and prayers, after seeing a guy come in and out of my room and smelling weed seeping from under my door all semester.

Despite these efforts, I still experienced some fear. Battling anxiety was a constant struggle. I couldn't sleep properly. My younger sister sent me YouTube meditations, and my mom even answered the phone in the middle of the night once and stayed on the line with me until she was at work at 8:00 am. I didn't think she would understand what I was going through, so when she picked up, I simply told her I was anxious and asked if we could read the book of Isaiah together. As I started speed reading, she asked me what was really troubling me. I just confessed, "I'm going through spiritual warfare because of the tarot reading." She tried to reassure me that everything would be fine, but the truth was that I was literally fighting demons. I made the decision to move back home early. Since classes were online, it wouldn't be a problem. I needed to leave that dorm as soon as possible. Silly enough, I was so paranoid that I felt like the YouTube tarot readers were haunting me through astral projection.

TEST 2: SMOKING WEED

At that time, it had been a while since I had smoked weed because I didn't have any. However, I had a friend who smoked, and whenever we hung out, she would offer me weed, and I always turned her down. I realized that I was starting to hurt her feelings, so this time, I decided to say yes. Little did I know it would be the last time I smoked. We went outside, and I took a few hits from her blunt. But this high was different, far from enjoyable. My heart was racing, and I started hallucinating. As my heart was beating so fast I started hearing things. It's like I was watching myself go insane from outside of my body. On the surface I tried my best to keep cool. In my head, I prayed and begged God to make me sober again. I promised myself I would never smoke again, and eventually, the high wore off. I was deeply disappointed. I had hoped that my last high would be just as fun as the previous ones, but it turned out to be a horrible experience. Well, no more weed for me. I don't know what would've happened if I had kept watching porn, but I know from these experiences it wouldn't have been good.

As we grow through life, regardless of our age or whether we are followers of Christ, it's easy to reflect on our past and think, "What was I thinking?" When I look back at the things I used to do, how I used to behave, the company I kept, and all the time I wasted, I now realize that if I had Jesus in my life during those moments, those things would have never happened. If only I had known. If only that veil over my heart hadn't deceived me.

Now that the veil has been lifted, I understand that even though I see the world differently, the world is still under their own perception. God has given us the ability to see that darkness and evil don't necessarily appear as monsters; they often disguise themselves as ordinary things we used to find comfort in. Suddenly, when people express feelings of being lost, depressed, and anxious, you can see how they keep themselves trapped in that torment through their own lifestyle choices. You begin to clearly see light from darkness. The light is Jesus, and the darkness is the world controlled by the Kingdom of darkness. There is no middle ground.

> Jesus spoke to the people and said, "I am the light of the world. If you follow me, you won't have to walk in darkness because you will have the light that leads to life."
>
> John 8:12 NLT

TEMPTATION

> I don't really understand myself, for I want to do what is right, but I don't do it. Instead, I do what I hate. But if I know that what I am doing is wrong, this shows that I agree that the law is good. So I am not the one doing wrong; it is sin living in me that does it. And I know that nothing good lives in me, that is, in my sinful nature. I want to do what is right, but I can't. I want to do what is good, but I don't. I don't want to do what is wrong, but I end up doing it anyway. And if I do what I don't want to do, I am not really the one doing wrong; it is sin living in me that does it.
>
> Romans 7:15–20 NLT

Although we can see clearly now, it doesn't change the fact that we are human. We may be children of God but we are not invincible.

Our flesh may be buried, but it still cries out, tempting us to join forces with it once again. The things we used to do continue to haunt us, and sometimes we may stumble and fall. Following Christ doesn't change the fact that we are still weak, but that's precisely why we must follow Him. With Him, we have the Holy Spirit who can help us overcome temptation. The Lord knows that we will be tempted, so temptation itself is not inherently bad; it's expected. He rejoices when we conquer it and choose to use our free will for good.

Naturally, we all experience temptations in our own flesh, but the enemy will go even further to increase the frequency of these temptations in our lives, especially when we're pursuing righteousness. That's why it's crucial for us to remain vigilant. During my first year of college, I used to party a lot, but I didn't face many lustful temptations during those outings. However, things changed in my second year. I don't mention this to boast, but after I committed my life to Christ, I noticed that I was receiving more male attention.

As a hairstylist trying to grow my clientele on campus, most of my initial clients were attractive male student athletes. At the time, I enjoyed the validation and attention, but I wasn't spiritually mature enough to understand that the enemy was trying to lead me astray with temptations I had never encountered before. I had given him direct access to tempt me. Dealing with lust became much more complicated after that. I had now experienced the thrill of entertaining boys whom I had no business seeing in the long run. Sometimes, I even felt the desire to go out and get drunk just to feel confident enough to flirt, seeking male validation that I had never received. I would even sit in the car while my friends smoked weed, even though I had quit, because I didn't want to be rude and get out. I'd also listen to their wild hookup stories, as if I wasn't an abstinent virgin fighting against lust. At some point, I had to establish boundaries, and when I wasn't strong enough to do it myself, God intervened. There would be instances when I'd on my way to meet a guy, and he would cancel on me right after I had just got all cute. I would plan to attend a party only for it to be randomly canceled or ending two hours early before I got there. Many old friends just stopped inviting me to hang out, leaving me with a sense of abandonment, but it was God saving me from myself once again.

> He himself has gone through suffering and testing, so he is able to help us when we are being tested.
>
> Hebrews 2:18 NLT

The Bible advises us against certain things to grant us freedom from sin and make it easier to overcome temptation. Although the Bible was written about 3400 years ago, it doesn't specifically mention things like marijuana, secular entertainment, and pornography. However, the scriptures indirectly suggest that these things can be categorized as lacking sober-mindedness and engaging in sexual immorality. Being sober-minded encompasses more than just abstaining from getting drunk or high. It's essential to be cautious about what we see, hear, and the environments we expose ourselves to since they can directly lead to temptation. Watching secular movies or listening to secular music is not inherently sinful, but these forms of entertainment can have a negative influence if they promote lust, sexual immorality, drug use, wild partying, or toxic behavior, especially if these are areas in which we personally struggle. It doesn't make sense to make the fight against sin more challenging by entertaining the idea of it through the content we consume. Sitting in such environments opens direct gateways, that allow the enemy to come into our lives and make the battle against sin even harder.

> But put on the Lord Jesus Christ, and make no provision for the flesh, to gratify its desires.
>
> Romans 13:14 ESV

CONVICTION

> For the kind of sorrow God wants us to experience leads us away from sin and results in salvation. There's no regret for that kind of sorrow. But worldly sorrow, which lacks repentance, results in spiritual death.
>
> 2 Corinthians 7:10 NLT

Before God closes a door in our face, He always convicts us. Conviction comes from the Holy Spirit and corrects us when we engage in activities we know we shouldn't, ultimately calling us to a higher standard. Conviction from God is similar to the correction and discipline our parents provide while we're growing up. It may not feel pleasant to be told by God that our actions are wrong, but it's ultimately for our own good. God cares about us so much, that He will not let us indulge in whatever we desire without experiencing the consequences. That's what the devil does. <u>When we engage in worldly things, the enemy allows us to comfortably remain in sin because we're doing exactly what he wants us to do, but he will ultimately abandon us to the consequences they bring.</u> When we asked God to be with us, we also asked Him to correct us when we're wrong and prevent us from returning to the broad path of sin.

After learning that wild parties were sinful in a Bible study, I felt convicted every time I went out. For me, it manifested as anxiety—a tight feeling in my chest and constant conflicting thoughts. God started unsettling my spirit and making me uncomfortable each time I prepared to go out because He didn't want me to be there. I realized what I had been doing was wrong, but I initially denied the conviction and made excuses. When we persist in living in sin while walking with God, it becomes challenging to enjoy that sin like we used to. We can no longer blissfully exist in ignorance. God will continue making us more and more uncomfortable whenever we reject conviction until we finally listen to Him.

Some of us may find ourselves convicted by certain things while other believers have no issue with them. This often arises when discussing topics like secular music, moderate alcohol consumption, and the boundaries of modesty. <u>If something is a sin, it remains so regardless of whether we feel convicted or not.</u>

However, some people may have stricter personal boundaries than others. I've been in situations where I adopted someone else's conviction as my own, and when I expressed my concerns to God, He called me a Pharisee—someone who is overly religious and self-righteous. I burdened myself with something that God hadn't asked me to carry, and it didn't make me any holier; it just stressed me out. Even if we personally feel that something is wrong, we should not impose our convictions on others. However, when we feel that something is wrong in our own lives, it is wrong for us to continue partaking in it, regardless of whether other believers can engage in it without guilt or not.

> You may believe there's nothing wrong with what you are doing, but keep it between yourself and God. Blessed are those who don't feel guilty for doing something they have decided is right. But if you have doubts about whether or not you should eat something, you are sinning if you go ahead and do it. For you are not following your convictions. If you do anything you believe is not right, you are sinning.
>
> Romans 14:22–23 NLT

It's easy to confuse conviction, which is good, with condemnation, which is bad. When I first encountered condemnation shortly after giving my life to Christ, I experienced an overwhelming sense of shame and guilt from my past. It made me feel unworthy of God's love and hindered my progress because I believed I had disappointed Him. It felt like every time I tried to improve, the enemy would come into my mind and remind me of my mistakes, never allowing me to forget them. The thoughts I had were self-defeating and paralyzing. Those feelings did not come from God. Condemnation is sent by the enemy to make us feel unforgivable, but it's a lie. Nothing can separate us from God's love. After all, He sent His Son to die for us. The moment we repent, God casts our sins into "the sea of forgetfulness" (Micah 7:19), and His love keeps no record of our wrongdoings. So, why should we hold them against ourselves?

And have you forgotten the encouraging words God spoke to you as his children? He said, "My child, don't make light of the Lord 's discipline, and don't give up when he corrects you. For the Lord disciplines those he loves, and he punishes each one he accepts as his child." As you endure this divine discipline, remember that God is treating you as his own children. Who ever heard of a child who is never disciplined by its father? If God doesn't discipline you as he does all of his children, it means that you are illegitimate and are not really his children at all. Since we respected our earthly fathers who disciplined us, shouldn't we submit even more to the discipline of the Father of our spirits, and live forever? For our earthly fathers disciplined us for a few years, doing the best they knew how. But God's discipline is always good for us, so that we might share in his holiness. No discipline is enjoyable while it is happening—it's painful! But afterward there will be a peaceful harvest of right living for those who are trained in this way.

Hebrews 12:5–11 NLT

CHAPTER SEVEN

REBIRTH.

A few weeks after enduring the most isolated period of my life, my parents came to help me move out of my dorm. I was eager to leave room 1111 behind, hoping that no one else would suffer like I did.

I was determined to get my life back on track and find healing. I prayed for God to restore everything that had been taken from me. I longed for genuine friendships instead of frenemies and accomplices, true love instead of situationships, and the restoration of my joy and peace. Letting go of those who hurt me took longer than I care to admit, and it felt embarrassing in the eyes of the world. No matter how many times I told myself to let it go, I couldn't help but hold onto the hope of rekindling my situationship and reminisce on times with my black friends and Judas. However, God didn't want me to be ashamed or embarrassed about the way I loved and forgave others so easily. Instead, He wanted me to embrace it. He taught me to pray for them.

Instead of delving into tarot readings, I immersed myself in Christian YouTube content. I spent my days and nights watching videos, even playing them like podcasts while working. I watched Ashley Empowers who taught me to approach dating with a balanced perspective, avoiding over-spiritualization while building and maintaining healthy standards. I watched LoveYourNatural who brought me out of my naive ways by empowering me to assert myself, set boundaries, and stop allowing boys to toy with my emotions. The "Everything is We" podcast with Cam and Vicky Logan showed me what a healthy, God-centered relationship could look like, full of youth and fun. Breeny Lee taught me the importance of self-worth, confidence, and cultivating inner value as a woman. All of their videos had a profound impact on my life, but one in particular left an unforgettable impression. It was a video by Alyssa of Wonderful Acts that would change my life forever, as she baptized me with the Holy Spirit through a TV screen. I had been binge watching her discipleship series and I remember this one video very distinctly.

"BAPTISM OF THE HOLY SPIRIT || Discipleship Series (Part 6)"

Sitting at the edge of my bed, captivated by Alyssa's words on the screen, I was surrounded by the beauty of a typical sunny day in

California. From my second-story bedroom window, I could see the neighborhood with a few queen palm trees swaying in the wind and a direct view of the sunset. As the video neared its end, Alyssa extended an invitation to her viewers to receive the baptism of the Holy Spirit

"I would love, I would be honored... Oh my gosh, so honored to pray with you right now to receive the baptism of the Holy Spirit. Yes, right now. I know if we were in person you'd be like right now? Here? In Starbucks? Yes. Let's do it," she said.

She instructed us to close our eyes, open our hands in a posture of receiving, and be expectant. Uncertain of what to anticipate, as Alyssa began praying in tongues, I felt a similar "fear" to when I first heard God's voice, fearing that I too would start speaking in a heavenly language. I decided to lie on my back as she led us in a prayer to receive the Holy Spirit. It's hard to put into words, but I felt refreshed. It was the same sensation I experience today when I seek God's comfort through prayer. There were no floating sensations or angelic encounters this time, but something changed within my spirit.

So, there I was, having given my life to Christ through a YouTube sermon, received deliverance from a demonic spirit over the phone, and now had been baptized with the Holy Spirit through a YouTube video. The Gen-Z followers of Christ are indeed a unique generation. Now, it was time for me to embark on the journey of transformation. Becoming a new creation is an ongoing process, as there is always something within ourselves that requires work.

During that time, my mind was tormented by intrusive dark thoughts that I knew weren't my own. Going to bed alone made me feel incredibly vulnerable, as it transported me back to my dorm room, where I feared having to fight demons once again. Disturbing thoughts, too dark to repeat, would invade my mind. I was deeply concerned. I recognized it as a mental attack and would rebuke each thought, but it was exhausting. I felt tormented. I can't explain why it took me so long to find peace in my own bedroom. It seemed that when I was alone, the enemy would mock me, knowing I wasn't fully equipped to defend myself spiritually. Every night, I slept in my big sister's room, sometimes sharing laughs while watching old black sitcoms, and other times crying in her arms as she prayed over me. It was the most nurturing side of her I had ever witnessed.

BECOMING NEW

> Jesus replied, "I tell you the truth, unless you are born again, you cannot see the Kingdom of God." "What do you mean?" exclaimed Nicodemus. "How can an old man go back into his mother's womb and be born again?" Jesus replied, "I assure you, no one can enter the Kingdom of God without being born of water and the Spirit. Humans can reproduce only human life, but the Holy Spirit gives birth to spiritual life. So don't be surprised when I say, "You must be born again."
>
> John 3:3–7 NLT

Although we are born into sin, each one of us starts with a pure and innocent mind. However, as time goes by, our minds become corrupted by the ways of the world. When we don't prioritize God's agenda in our lives, the enemy takes the opportunity to influence us.

This is why it is crucial for us to experience a spiritual rebirth. We often fall into the habit of conforming to the world's behaviors and customs, so we must allow God to renew our minds, restore our purity (Romans 12:2), and humble us, making us childlike once more.

When people asked Jesus about becoming born again, they took His words too literally. We don't physically return to our mother's womb through a hospital trip. It's not a physical rebirth. No external changes to our bodies can alter our spirits. No amount of cosmetic surgery, hair extensions, or Instagram likes can renew us or mold us into righteous individuals worthy of entering the Kingdom of God. Instead, we must allow the Holy Spirit to "give birth to spiritual life" within us. It marks the beginning of a new life, where we walk in the spirit rather than in the flesh, which had been our way of life until then.

Being born of water refers to baptism in the name of the Father, Son, and Holy Spirit. It serves as an outward expression of the inward birth of our spiritual life. It symbolizes our decision to dedicate our lives to Christ. I personally underwent baptism twice. The first time was during my childhood when my mother had me baptized along with other kids at our church. We formed a line against the wall after the service and took turns being immersed in the large swimming pool on the stage. I remember wanting to wear a swimsuit, but my mom insisted I wear the same black full-body leotard we used under our costumes during praise dance performances. I had no understanding of what was happening. The second time I was baptized, I was 19 years old, after my sophomore year of college. It had been a year and a half since I rededicated my life to Christ. I had been attending a church near my college campus, and I postponed getting baptized throughout the school year. I was waiting for my family to visit me in college or for a friend group of believers who understood my experiences to instantly appear. I was even waiting for my hair to be in old box braids, so I wouldn't have to watch it revert back to its natural 4c curls in front of everyone. I wanted people present who could testify to the transformation they witnessed in my life. But my waiting was in vain. It felt as if I were hearing God's voice, singing to me in Bob Marley's tone, "I don't wanna wait in vain for your love...". I started questioning why I had waited for so long. God had the power to transform me even without baptism, and indeed He did. There was no reason for me to wait for mere people to validate my relationship with Him.

> If you come to me but will not leave your family, you cannot be my follower. You must love me more than your father, mother, wife, children, brothers, and sisters—even more than your own life!
>
> Luke 14:26 ERV

By the end of summer, I came to the realization that the presence of others didn't matter because my relationship with God was personal. I dedicated my life to Him <u>alone</u> in my dorm room, attended my small church <u>alone</u> every Sunday, and pursued Him <u>alone</u> in isolation on a daily basis. I literally would have dunked myself in the bathtub and baptized myself if I could've. So, I finally did it. At that time, I had already cut my hair short, embracing my 4c curls so I didn't have to worry about it shriveling up in front of everyone. Surprisingly, even though I had only engaged in small talk with the church members, they had such positive things to say about what they had observed in me simply by seeing me at church every Sunday. The act of baptism didn't have to be a grand, picturesque event for social media. It just needed to be done.

I often questioned the validity of my experience of coming to Christ because it differs significantly from that of the typical believer. One reason is that the world wouldn't necessarily label my testimony as diabolical like Paul's, or extremely intense, involving homelessness or coming from a broken home. However, it would have led to the same outcome of being told, "Depart from me, I never knew you." And even though I have left that place, there are many people like me who are still there. The other reason is that 90% of my journey with Christ has been spent behind closed doors, in front of screens (TV, phone, earbuds), and now behind a microphone and camera since starting a YouTube channel. Up to this point, I have never experienced a traditional altar call, never received a prophetic message from a fellow church member, never shared my testimony in front of a congregation, and I struggle to make friends at church. I only questioned it once, and I will never doubt it again. The reality and intimacy of God are not limited by any constraints. He works through everything. He strategically wrote my story in this way. It's unique, and I prefer it this way. I am no different because my strongest moments of worship aren't confined to Sunday mornings at church, or because my most intimate prayers aren't always done when the pastor says, "Bow your heads, close your eyes." My God is not confined to a building; He is continuously within me.

> Don't let anyone call you 'Rabbi,' for you have only one teacher, and all of you are equal as brothers and sisters. And don't address anyone here on earth as 'Father,' for only God in heaven is your Father. And don't let anyone call you 'Teacher,' for you have only one teacher, the Messiah.
>
> Matthew 23:8–10 NLT

Becoming new is a literal transformation that occurs. Many people don't recognize themselves after they give their lives to Christ. As we shed the old, lifeless things, we begin to embrace the things of God that bring us true life. We truly become new creations, new individuals. Our identity is found entirely in Christ. Paul even received a new name. Personally, I dyed my hair a new color. Not only did I not recognize myself, but old friends from my hometown, family members, and fellow churchgoers couldn't stop commenting on how different I looked and seemed. I had to reintroduce myself to friends who hadn't really gotten to know this new version of me, and they had to meet me again as a transformed individual who no longer acted like the old me. When I look at old photos and videos, it feels as though I'm looking at someone else's life. Seeing them now is shocking because the person I am today wouldn't have been friends with the person I used to be.

We mourn the things of the past, but they are indeed dead and must remain that way. Our previous lifestyle, friends, and habits will not accompany us on our journey forward, nor will our former tendencies, behaviors, and mannerisms. God now shapes us like clay, removing hindrances, applying pressure, and carefully sculpting new versions of ourselves. We have been resurrected with Him after burying our old selves. Although we will never attain His level of perfection, it provides us with plenty to work on.

GROWING WITH GOD

> Put on your new nature, and be renewed as you learn to know your Creator and become like him.
>
> Colossians 3:10 NLT

Establishing a relationship with God is similar to building a friendship or a romantic connection. Just as we spend time with someone, listen to their voice, and talk to them, Colossians 3 instructs us to get to know our Creator. If we dedicate our lives to God without following up with Him, transformational growth becomes unlikely. The pace of our progress varies based on our level of devotion, obedience, and willingness, but we are continually being perfected as we strive to imitate His nature. Each day, we are refined and called to a higher standard than the previous day.

To become more like Christ, it is essential to understand who He is and how He lived. This understanding comes from reading the Word and familiarizing ourselves with His character. Merely attending church on Sundays will not suffice for developing a strong relationship with God. He desires our time and attention. He is a jealous God, not in the sense of envying what we possess, but in desiring our attention above all else. Just as we willingly gave in to sin, we should eagerly and promptly give our attention to God. He simply wants to hear our voices every day. He wants us to find rest in Him, rather than seeking solace in self-care activities. Moreover, He wants to be the first person we turn to in times of adversity. Our priority should be seeking His righteousness and His kingdom above all else, placing so much faith in Him that we trust He will provide for all our needs (Matthew 6:33). Our relationship with God should be the one reliable thing that never disappoints us. It should develop into a solid foundation that remains unshaken in the face of challenges. While God did not promise a perfect, pain-free life, He did promise to be with us through every storm.

The same spirit that raised Christ from the dead now resides within us, and it is our responsibility to allow the Holy Spirit to guide our lives. We should exemplify the fruits of the Spirit - love, joy, peace, patience, kindness, goodness, faithfulness, gentleness, and self-control - as evidence of His presence in us. Our bodies should become temples for the Holy Spirit. Growth in our relationship with God occurs through intentional habits we cultivate to draw closer to Him. These habits include daily reading of the Word, spending time in prayer, and deepening our intimacy with Him through worship.

NARROW PATH

> You can enter God's Kingdom only through the narrow gate. The highway to hell is broad, and its gate is wide for the many who choose that way. But the gateway to life is very narrow and the road is difficult, and only a few ever find it.
>
> Matthew 7:13–14 NLT

Choosing to give our lives to Christ means transitioning from the broad path to the narrow path. While the broad path leads to destruction, it is convenient and easier to find companionship on it. However, the narrow path is different. It is described as difficult in the scriptures, implying that it requires significant effort to walk on. Nevertheless, the reward far outweighs the challenges. The suffering we experience on this path cannot be compared to the glory that will be revealed to us in the future (Romans 8:18). The narrow path can be lonely, especially without a solid Christian community for support. As I navigate this narrow path during my college years, barely approaching my twenties, I have encountered considerable hardship. There is a false notion perpetuated that being a believer makes life perfect, but it is precisely the opposite of what the Bible teaches. I refuse to reinforce these lies. Figuring out how to live as a young Christian adult has been extremely challenging. While the Lord wants us to enjoy our lives, He doesn't want us to engage in foolish activities. With the "college experience" often promoting wild parties, hookup culture, and the trendy wave of New Age Spirituality, I frequently felt like I couldn't enjoy myself because the things I desired didn't involve getting under the influence of substances or engaging in casual sex. I struggled internally with God every time I received invitations to parties, knowing I shouldn't go, but not wanting to be alone and bored. I battled with Him each time a charming athlete asked me to hang out, aware that their intentions were purely physical. Now I realize that God didn't want me to be lonely; He simply wanted me to find activities I enjoy apart from the world, for my own well-being. He didn't want the world to hurt me again by involving me with people and things that would only bring pain. He did not want to witness me going through that anguish. Why should I give the devil an opportunity to abandon me again?

However, despite these realizations, I still feel like an outsider. We are called to live in this world but remain distinct from it. We adhere to a different set of values that the world does not abide by. I often pleaded with God for just one person who understood me, who loved Him as much as I did and genuinely walked with Him. Most of my loneliness did not stem from missing the broad path; rather, I longed for a companion to walk alongside me on the narrow path. Throughout this time I begged God for a relationship or a best friend, and in His temporary denial, He showed me that He had occupied that position all along. I had relied on people to validate my lifestyle throughout my life, and it was time to let Him be the sole audience. It was time to relinquish my dependence on unreliable individuals and truly lean on Him for companionship.

In these moments of isolation on this narrow path, He continues to reveal my passions and purpose for this life. He uncovers aspects of myself that I would never have discovered if I had continued on the broad path, surrounded by various influences sowing doubt in my mind. I now find joy in solitude with Him. Even if no one else ever knows or witnesses my journey, I can rest assured that He has scripted every detail and guided me every step of the way. There was no way for me to "find myself" on the broad path. <u>It is on the narrow path that I discovered my identity is entirely in Christ, and He has already found me</u>. I simply need to follow Him, even when difficulties and suffering arise. The more I discover Him, the more I discover myself.

CHAPTER EIGHT

FREEDOM.

> So Christ has truly set us free. Now make sure that you stay free, and don't get tied up again in slavery to the law.
>
> Galatians 5:1 NLT

It is a liberating experience to emerge triumphantly from sin, realizing that we are no longer bound by the things we once believed we could never escape. This truth is cherished during every act of worship with the Father and conveyed through every expression of heartfelt gratitude in prayer. God's gift of freedom is the embodiment of pure love, a precious blessing that should neither be taken for granted nor forsaken.

SAVED BY GRACE ≠ SAVED BY WORKS

As for me, may I never boast about anything except the cross of our Lord Jesus Christ. Because of that cross, my interest in this world has been crucified, and the world's interest in me has also died.

Galatians 6:14 NLT

It is tempting to attribute our journeys with Christ solely to our own merits. Society has taught us to have an ego and take pride in our achievements. However, with Christ, our only reason to boast should be Him. To take credit for our salvation as if we accomplished it entirely on our own undermines the fact that God sent His only Son to die for our freedom. Jesus Christ faced betrayal and hatred from many even before He was nailed to the cross. Prior to His death, He endured public humiliation and torture. Strapped to a block, He was beaten with nailed whips that tore His skin and inflicted deep wounds. A crown of thorns was placed on His head, causing blood to flow into His eyes. Then, He was forced to carry His own cross to His death, all the while enduring mockery and spitting. He suffered as He awaited His death, with nails hammered into His hands and feet, enduring unimaginable pain. He endured all of this for you and me, who have been set free by Him, despite having denied Him.

He was oppressed and afflicted, yet he did not open his mouth; he was led like a lamb to the slaughter, and as a sheep before its shearers is silent, so he did not open his mouth. By oppression and judgment he was taken away. Yet who of his generation protested? For he was cut off from the land of the living; for the transgression of my people he was punished. He was assigned a grave with the wicked, and with the rich in his death, though he had done no violence, nor was any deceit in his mouth. Yet it was the Lord's will to crush him and cause him to suffer, and though the Lord makes his life an offering for sin, he will see his offspring and prolong his days, and the will of the Lord will prosper in his hand.

Isaiah 53:7–10 NLT

If we place too much faith in ourselves for our salvation, we will find ourselves back in chains. Not the chains of sin, but the chains of religion that convince us that our salvation is a result of our own actions. No matter how liberated we may feel from sin, our salvation is only possible because Jesus fulfilled the law on our behalf, and it was freely given to us. While it is wonderful to be free from sin, our celebration should solely be because of His strength that made it possible. We can become as joyful as we want after "beating a porn addiction for 30 days" but those moments should not be about seeking praise; they should be moments of glorifying God. Being proud of ourselves for being free from sin sets us up for failure when we stumble again. In those moments of failure, we will sulk in disappointment and condemn ourselves, all because of pride, instead of turning to God for strength, as we should have done in the first place, because we unjustly placed the burden of salvation in our own hands. Living righteously is a result of the Holy Spirit working within us and will never be solely due to our own good deeds, discipline, or morality.

I do not treat the grace of God as meaningless. For if keeping the law could make us right with God, then there was no need for Christ to die.

Galatians 2:21 NLT

Claiming perfection puts us in a dangerous position because we become so focused on appearing righteous that we forget to actually live righteously. I believe American culture is to blame for this. They teach us to go to church in our "Sunday Best" instead of coming as we are, allowing the Word of God to refine us, placing the priority on appearing godly rather than living godly. As a result, we see many people in church who act holy but live differently outside the church. This hypocrisy is one of the reasons why Gen-Z has left the church. They feel judged because of the self-righteousness and judgment projected by the church. Jesus did not approve of the Pharisees; He referred to them as blind guides and hypocrites. He also said that those who exalt themselves will be humbled, while those who humble themselves will be exalted (Hebrews 23:12). It has never been about how good we are, because we are not good. It is His grace that is sufficient.

How foolish can you be? After starting your new lives in the Spirit, why are you now trying to become perfect by your own human effort? Have you experienced so much for nothing? Surely it was not in vain, was it?

Galatians 3:3–4 NLT

NOT TAKING ADVANTAGE OF HIS GRACE

Well then, should we keep on sinning so that God can show us more and more of his wonderful grace? Of course not! Since we have died to sin, how can we continue to live in it?

Romans 6:1–2 NLT

Although God is always good to us, it doesn't mean we should abuse His forgiveness by habitually and deliberately living in a sinful lifestyle. Doing so would forfeit our freedom in Him and return us to the chains of our flesh. In that case, we would still be slaves, making ourselves the masters of our lives. We would regress into old habits because we've grown comfortable with stagnation. It is natural to struggle, but if we consistently grow in our relationship with God, there is no reason to hold onto those sins. Holding on to them shows a lack of faith in our ability to be truly set free and remain free.

Once I realized that God was calling me to go deeper, I ghosted Him. I was afraid of commitment. I didn't want to face the reality that I couldn't be a "Closet Christian" anymore, hiding my faith and blending in with others. I wanted to love Him privately while keeping my love for the world as my "side chick." By avoiding Him, I could stay ignorant and escape the responsibility of being held to a higher standard, and I wouldn't have to carry the sorrow that comes with great knowledge. If I had continued down that path, God would have become the "side chick". I would have been hurt by the world again and crawled back to Him in tears. At the point I am now, if I were to go back to my old ways, I would be crucifying Him all over again. Even though I feel more secure in Him than ever, my imperfect nature sometimes makes me fear that I will do that to Him in the future when unexpected challenges arise. That's the reality. I would love to say that being on fire for God is an unquenchable fire, but it only stays lit if we stay close to Him. If distance grows, it's our fault, not God's. He doesn't forsake His children, however, He will abandon us to our ways if we choose to deliberately live apart from Him. I often pray that God will never allow me to drift so far that I become further from where I started. I have more faith in Him to hold onto me, than in myself to hold onto Him.

> For it is impossible for those who were once enlightened, and have tasted the heavenly gift, and have become partakers of the Holy Spirit, and have tasted the good word of God and the powers of the age to come, if they fall away, to renew them again to repentance, since they crucify again for themselves the Son of God, and put Him to an open shame.
>
> Hebrews 6:4–6 NKJV

BREAKIING SINFUL HABITS

This is why we need to be radical when it comes to sin. Knowing that sin places a barrier between us and God, there should be nothing stopping us from doing whatever it takes to overcome it. Jesus said in Matthew 5:27-30 that if our right hand causes us to sin, we should cut it off, and if our right eye causes us to sin, we should pluck it out and cast it away. He emphasized that it is better to lose one part of the body than to be condemned to hell entirely. I used to think it wasn't that serious, but it truly is. No sin or bad habit is worth the destruction of our souls. If we believe we have been set free, then we are free. If we believe that God has given us the power and scripture to overcome the chains of sin, then we can. It's as simple as that.

> So I say, let the Holy Spirit guide your lives. Then you won't be doing what your sinful nature craves.
>
> **Galatians 5:16 NLT**

God liberated the Israelites from slavery in Egypt, but they questioned why He had brought them there in the first place while they were on their way to the promised land. As foolish as the Israelites looked when we read it back, we're more similar to them than we think. When I felt like there was nothing better than a good smoke session that involved hitting a blunt that'd hit me back, God showed me that His peace, love and joy gives me an indescribable spiritual high that doesn't compare to weed. Weed made me smile and laugh for no reason, and now God wakes me up every morning with a silly grin on my face. Yet I didn't have to destroy my lungs or my bank account to get it. At one point, I believed that having a solid relationship with a guy who knew me completely, comforted me, and was there for me in every moment would be the ultimate satisfaction. However, I discovered the intimacy of God, and the only cost is full devotion. <u>Everything the world offers comes at a cost, whether it's a literal monetary price or the price of selling your soul</u>. If you believe that there's nothing better than indulging in your favorite sin, try relacing that time with seeking God for a bit, and you will never thirst for it again. Without getting to know God, it's difficult to understand what He has in store for us. He isn't just here to fulfill our wishes like a genie if we please Him. What He desires most is a relationship with us, which alone brings complete satisfaction and contentment in this life. As long as we seek fulfillment from the world, we will always be unsatisfied. No amount of success, pleasure, or sin can fulfill us. We will forever be starved and searching for more as long as we look everywhere but to Him.

WARFARE

Congratulations. By surrendering to Christ, you have made hell nervous. The devil hates us, straight up. Although I don't like talking about him, it's necessary. If God didn't warn us about the enemy's tactics we would've been in for a rude awakening. Professing that Jesus is our Savior with our mouths is one thing, but taking action threatens the kingdom of darkness. The enemy will do anything to hinder our transformation. It's an actual war, and the victor claims our souls.

> For we are not fighting against flesh-and-blood enemies, but against evil rulers and authorities of the unseen world, against mighty powers in this dark world, and against evil spirits in the heavenly places.
>
> Ephesians 6:12 NLT

Every believer experiences spiritual warfare, but we each face different temptations and challenges. Personally, I struggled with lust, weed, partying, and tarot readings, which is where the enemy targeted me. The devil hates to see us begin living for God and will stop at nothing to hinder our progress.

Spiritual warfare occurs in the spiritual realm but manifests itself in various physical ways. It includes battles in our minds, health, finances, relationships, and more. It also tests our faith. Do we still believe in God's goodness when the enemy throws the hardest curveballs? Not every situation is from the devil, and sometimes life is simply difficult. However, in spiritual warfare, the devil may request permission from God to test us and break our faith in Him, just as he asked to sift us like wheat.

We cannot engage in spiritual warfare using physical means. Although we may observe things falling apart in our lives, we should combat them through prayer, fasting, reading, and worship instead of relying on physical methods. In the physical realm, our only task is to face trials with strong character, without allowing them to change our approach to life. Rather than reacting with anger, we should utilize the fruits of the spirit, which include love, joy, peace, patience, kindness, goodness, faithfulness, gentleness, and self-control. Through prayer in the spiritual realm, we let the devil know that our faith remains unbroken and unwavering. It demonstrates our understanding that God is greater than any problem we face and enables us to speak life into every lie the enemy tries to use to bring us down. Intense warfare calls for intense combat.

Fasting allows us to seek God at a higher level, enabling us to see and hear Him more clearly. As we dedicate more time to meditating on the truth of His Word, it exposes the lies of the enemy. Consequently, the enemy finds it more difficult to break us down because his lies begin to appear more <u>detectable</u> and <u>obvious</u>. Praising and worshiping God can be particularly challenging during times of trouble. It is easy to praise God when things are going well, but praising Him during difficult times demonstrates spiritual maturity. It reveals our understanding that situations come and go, but God remains consistently good. Spending more time in worship confuses the enemy and strengthens our confidence and hope in the Lord. Jesus becomes magnified above all our troubles and trials.

It is important to recognize that the enemy will stop at nothing to defeat us. However, God has equipped us to stand against him. When the enemy comes, we should not run away. We have been given the authority to cast him down, using the belt of truth and the breastplate of God's righteousness. To remain prepared, we must also put on the shoes of peace, which equip us to proclaim the Good News. When the enemy throws fiery arrows, we should lift up our faith as a shield for protection. In the face of intrusive negative and dark thoughts, we must put on the helmet of salvation, taking every thought captive and making it submit to the word of God. Finally, we should take up the sword of the Spirit as our weapon and be ready to expose the enemy's lies with the truth. We should pray without ceasing, stay alert, and persist in our efforts (Ephesians 6:11-18).

As we walk forward in the light, we become threats to the kingdom of darkness. Our God-given light can guide others who were once like us out of darkness just as Jesus did for us. Let us encourage one another to remain firmly rooted in the truth and remind ourselves of Jesus' life and sacrifice daily.

Therefore, since we are surrounded by such a huge crowd of witnesses to the life of faith, let us strip off every weight that slows us down, especially the sin that so easily trips us up. And let us run with endurance the race God has set before us. We do this by keeping our eyes on Jesus, the champion who initiates and perfects our faith. Because of the joy awaiting him, he endured the cross, disregarding its shame. Now he is seated in the place of honor beside God's throne. Think of all the hostility he endured from sinful people; then you won't become weary and give up.

Hebrews 12:1–3 NLT

LET'S PRAY

Dear Heavenly Father,

We come before You today on behalf of the young adults of our generation. We seek Your intervention to restore our connection with You. Remove the veil that keeps us in darkness and reveal Your radiant light. Even if it is painful, show us the truth. Pull the rug of deception out from under our feet and allow us to land in Your arms. Reveal to us the schemes that the devil has been playing in our lives and put an end to them once and for all in the mighty name of Jesus.

Guide us away from the broad path driven by our flesh, the enemy, and the influences of others. Instead, hold our hand and lead us down the narrow path. When the world turns its back on us, demonstrate Your goodness, mercy, and renew our hope for a brighter future. Remind us that we are not condemned, but we are set free through You. Unveil Your true nature to us as our Savior, Redeemer, Friend, Father, and so much more. When we seek temporary gratifications, quench our thirst with Your oil.

Help us reconcile with You by putting our flesh to death and empowering us to resist its cries. Introduce us to the transformed versions of ourselves and teach us how to emulate Your character. May our spiritual journey be one of continuous growth. Liberate us from the grip of sin that relentlessly competes for our attention. Grant us wisdom, knowledge, and passion to share Your word with this lost and dying world. Shape us into beacons of light, just as You are. Ignite in us the desire and determination to fight the good fight, so that when our race is complete, we will hear those cherished words, "Well done, my good and faithful servant."

In the name of the Father, the Son, and the Holy Spirit,

AMEN.

NOTES

NOTES

NOTES

NOTES

NOTES

NOTES

NOTES

NOTES

NOTES

NOTES

FOLLOW @IAMJADACHRISTINE

RECENT YOUTUBE VIDEOS

TIKTOK

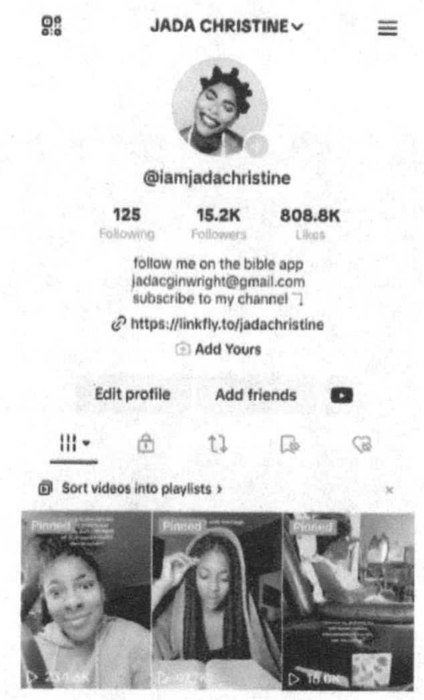